13/95

FROM LOGIC TO COMPUTERS

COMPUTER SCIENCE TEXTS

COMPUTER SCIENCE TEXTS

From Logic to Computers

P. J. THEWLIS
BSc, PhD, MBCS
School of Mathematics Computing and Statistics,
Leicester Polytechnic

B. N. T. FOXON
TD, BSc, PhD
School of Mathematics Computing and Statistics,
Leicester Polytechnic

BLACKWELL SCIENTIFIC PUBLICATIONS
OXFORD LONDON EDINBURGH
BOSTON MELBOURNE

Editorial offices:
Osney Mead, Oxford, OX2 0EL
8 John Street, London, WC1N 2ES
9 Forrest Road, Edinburgh, EH1 2QH
52 Beacon Street, Boston
Massachusetts 02108, USA
99 Barry Street, Carlton
Victoria 3053, Australia

First published 1983

Phototypeset by
Parkway Illustrated Press, Abingdon

Printed and bound in Great Britain at the Alden Press, Oxford

British Library
Cataloguing in Publication Data

Thewlis, P. J.
From logic to computers.—(Computer science texts)
1. Logic circuits 2. Electronic digital computers—Circuits
I. Title II. Foxon, B. N. T III. Series
621.3819'5835 TK7888.4

ISBN 0-632-01183-1

Contents

Introduction

The aim of this book is to introduce computer hardware to the computer enthusiast as well as to computer science and information technology students. No specialist knowledge of electronics or computing is required or assumed. The book starts with a very simple introduction to logic gates and builds up through combinational logic circuits to the design of a simple arithmetic and logic unit. Sequential logic is then introduced and the design of simple circuits for use in a digital computer are described.

The combinational and sequential logic circuits are used in the overall design of a simple computer. Using this, the concepts of stored programs, machine code instructions and the execution of machine code programs are explained.

The final chapter relates the designs developed throughout the book to large-scale integrated circuits and microprocessors.

The book has been designed as a stand-alone text. The reader will, however, gain invaluable practical experience by constructing the logic tutor described in Appendix 2, carrying out the practical exercises in Appendix 3 and building the circuits developed throughout the text. The logic tutor uses only standard components which are available from most electronics component suppliers.

The authors would like to thank Motorola Ltd for permission to redraw information from their publication, *Microcomputer System Design Book* (1976), for Figs 9.3, 9.4, 9.5, 9.10 and 9.11, and Zilog (UK) Ltd for permission to redraw information from their publication, *Zilog 1981 Data Book* (1981) for Figs 9.6 and 9.7. (Motorola reserves the right to make any changes to any products herein to improve reliability, function or design. Motorola does not assume any liability arising out of the application or use of any product or circuit described herein; neither does it convey any license under its patent rights nor the rights of others.)

The authors would also like to express their gratitude to their colleagues Steve Rumsby, Martin Lefley and Brian Clarke for their help and to acknowledge the support and encouragement they have received from their wives Carolyn and Pauline, who also typed the manuscript.

Chapter 1

Logic Gates

1.1 INTRODUCTION

Since the advent of numbers human beings have been working in decimal, probably because they have ten fingers. Unfortunately, computers have no fingers and work solely by means of the presence or lack of an electrical signal. In other words, something being either on or off, a voltage being present or not. It is usual to denote the presence of a signal with the number 1 and the lack of a signal by the number 0. This is called binary and forms the basis of all digital computers. One of the simplest forms of binary circuit is a switch with a battery and lamp as shown in Fig. 1.1.

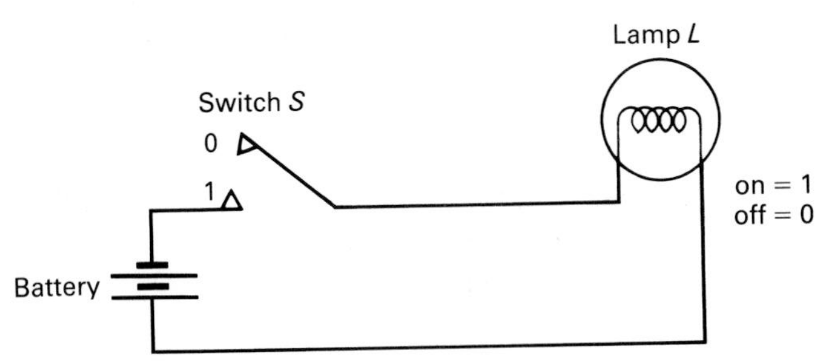

Fig. 1.1. ASSERTION circuit.

The switch when closed can represent a logical 1 and when open a logical 0. In other words the switch is used to represent a binary input to the circuit.

The lamp when on can represent a logical 1 and when off a logical 0, i.e. the lamp can be used to represent the binary output from the circuit.

The operation of this circuit can then be summarized using a *truth table* (a table showing the state of each output for every combination of inputs), as shown in Table 1.1.

This logical function is called ASSERTION.

In the mid-nineteenth century, logical or Boolean algebra was developed by George Boole to simplify complex logical propositions. Nowadays Boolean algebra plays a significant part in the analysis and logical design of computer systems. The Boolean representation of assertion is $L = S$.

Table 1.1

S	L
0	0
1	1

The following three switch lamp circuits demonstrate the prime logical functions of NEGATION, AND and OR. These functions cannot be simplified further and form the basis of all logic circuitry.

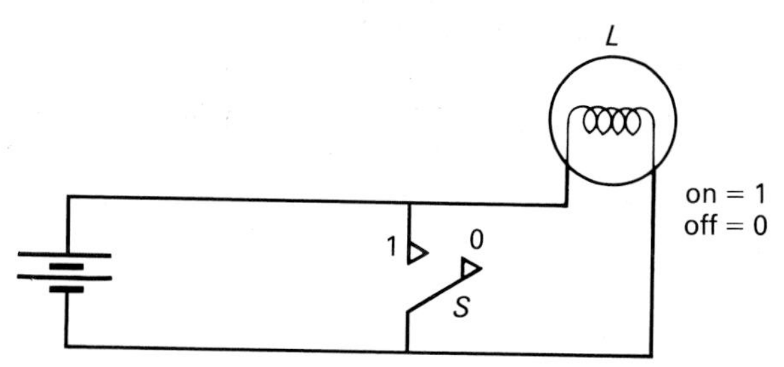

Fig. 1.2. NEGATION circuit.

NEGATION

With the switch closed (logical 1) the current flows through the switch and the lamp is off. With the switch open the lamp is on.

The operation can be represented by the truth table shown in Table 1.2.

Table 1.2

S	L
0	1
1	0

This logical function is called NEGATION and is represented in Boolean algebra by the expression $L = \overline{S}$, (the bar signifying negation or inversion).

AND

Consider a circuit with two switches and a lamp in series as shown in Fig. 1.3. With both switches in the closed position (i.e. logical 1) the lamp is on (representing a logical 1). With any other combination of inputs the lamp is off (logical 0). The truth table for this circuit is shown in Table 1.3.

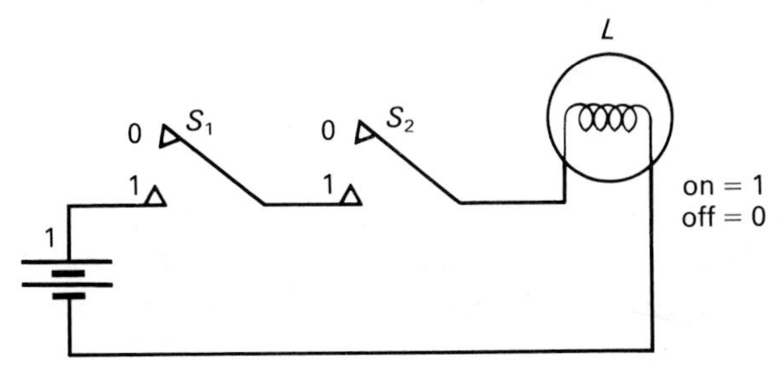

Fig. 1.3. AND gate circuit.

Table 1.3

S_1	S_2	L
0	0	0
1	0	0
0	1	0
1	1	1

This is the logical function, AND, and is represented in Boolean algebra by $L = S_1.S_2$ ($L = 1$ when S_1 *and* $S_2 = 1$). (Note: the '.' sign signifies the logical function AND.)

OR

With the two switches in parallel the circuit becomes that shown in Fig. 1.4. The truth table for this circuit is shown in Table 1.4. This is the logical function, OR, and is represented in Boolean algebra by $L = S_1 + S_2$ ($L = 1$ when either S_1 *or* S_2 *or* both are 1). (Note: the '+' sign signifies the logical function, OR.

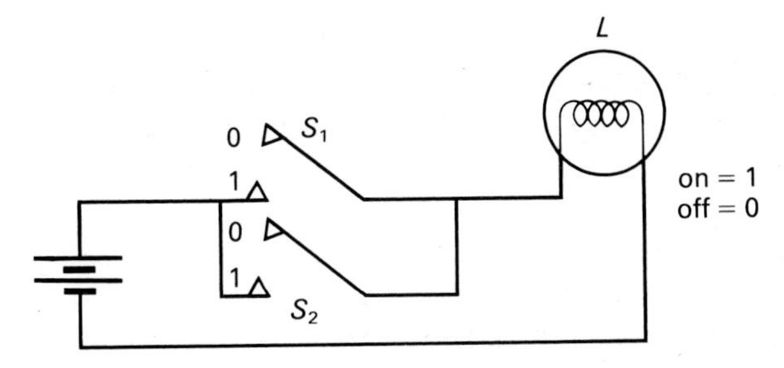

Fig. 1.4. OR gate circuit.

These three prime logical functions form the basis of all complex logic functions. It is common practice to combine two of these functions together to form NAND and NOR functions. The following switch and lamp circuits illustrate these functions.

Table 1.4

S_1	S_2	L
0	0	0
1	0	1
0	1	1
1	1	1

NOR

The circuit shown in Fig. 1.5 with the switches in series but with their logical designations inverted illustrates the NOR function. The truth table for this circuit is shown in Table 1.5.

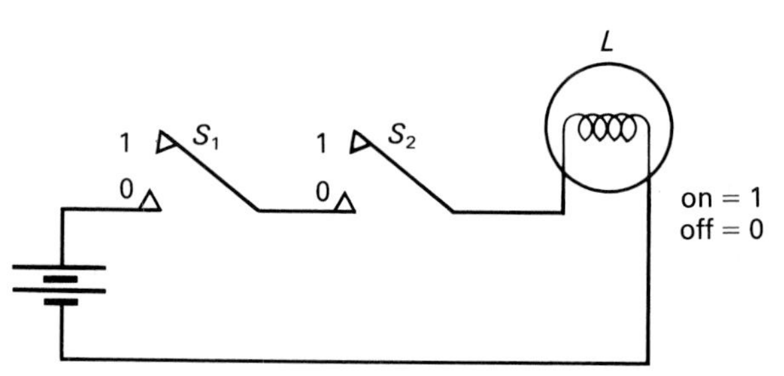

Fig. 1.5. NOR gate circuit.

Table 1.5

S_1	S_2	L
0	0	1
1	0	0
0	1	0
1	1	0

It can be seen that the output from this circuit is equivalent to that of the OR circuit negated. This logical function is called the Negated OR or NOR and is represented in Boolean algebra by the expression $L = \overline{S_1 + S_2}$.

NAND

With the two switches in parallel and the designation of switch position inverted the circuit becomes that shown in Fig. 1.6. The truth table for this circuit is shown in Table 1.6.

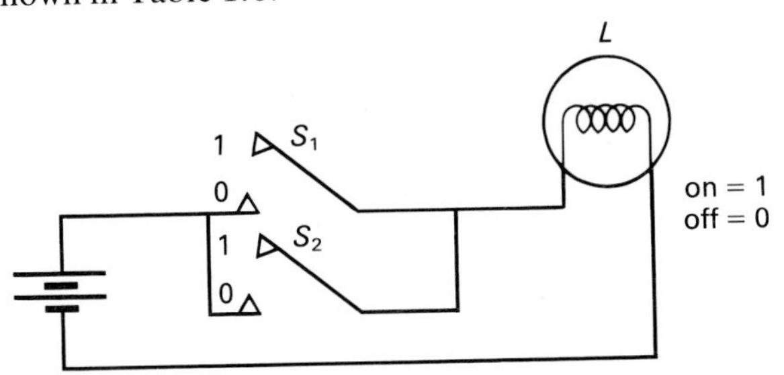

Fig. 1.6. NAND gate circuit.

Table 1.6

S_1	S_2	L
0	0	1
1	0	1
0	1	1
1	1	0

It can be seen that the output from this circuit is equivalent to that of the AND circuit negated. This logical function is called the Negated AND or NAND and is represented in Boolean algebra by the expression $L = \overline{S_1.S_2}$.

These five logical functions can be summarized as shown in Table 1.7.

Table 1.7

Function	Boolean algebra
NEGATION	$\overline{S}_1$
AND	$S_1.S_2$
OR	$S_1 + S_2$
NAND	$\overline{S_1.S_2}$
NOR	$\overline{S_1 + S_2}$

1.2 LOGIC GATES

The elementary switching circuits illustrated above are clearly of little use since they rely on manual operation of the switches. In order to build logic circuits automatic switching must be employed.

Relays, switches which close when an electric current is applied, could be used in place of the manual switches. For example, the OR circuit described above is shown in Fig. 1.7.

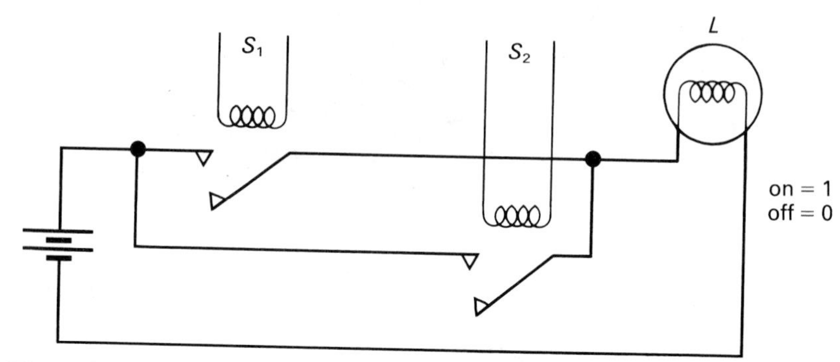

Fig. 1.7. Relay implementation of OR circuit.

By defining the no signal state as an 0 and the signal state as a 1 on the inputs S_1 and S_2 and on the Lamp L, an OR gate can be produced.

When a signal is present on S_1 or S_2 or both the appropriate relay(s) are energized causing the switch to close and the lamp to be switched on.

The first logic elements were of the relay type, however, relays are slow, expensive and bulky and with advances in electronics much smaller and faster logic circuits were produced using, initially discrete transistors and in more recent times integrated circuits.

1.3 COMMON LOGIC ELEMENTS

Integrated circuits contain a number of logic gates, ranging from three or four in simple chips to many thousands in more complex parts. To enable logic elements to be represented in schematic form the following notation was developed. This notation was initially used for defence contracts in the United States, and is now a widely accepted standard.

An INVERTER

Schematic representation

A (input) → INVERTER → B (output)

Boolean algebra

$B = \bar{A}$

Truth table

A	B
0	1
1	0

Fig. 1.8. An INVERTER.

AND gates

Schematic representation	Boolean algebra	Truth table
A, B inputs; C output	$C = A.B$	

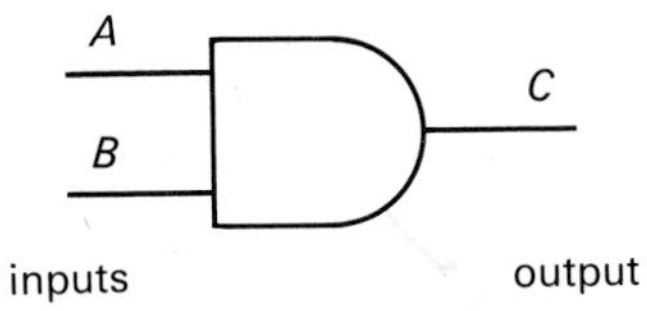

A	B	C
0	0	0
0	1	0
1	0	0
1	1	1

Fig. 1.9. A two input AND gate.

Figure 1.9 represents a two input AND gate and the truth table shows the output C for the four possible combinations of the inputs A and B.

Logic gates can have several inputs. Figure 1.10 shows a three input AND gate and its associated truth table. The truth table gives the output D for each of the eight possible combinations of the inputs A, B and C.

Schematic representation	Boolean algebra	Truth table
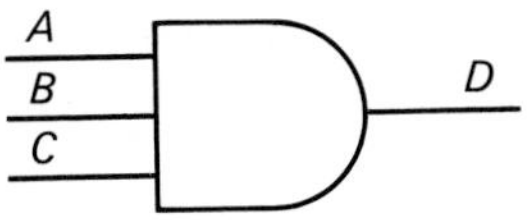 A, B, C inputs; D output	$D = A.B.C$	

A	B	C	D
0	0	0	0
0	0	1	0
0	1	0	0
0	1	1	0
1	0	0	0
1	0	1	0
1	1	0	0
1	1	1	1

Fig. 1.10. A three input AND gate.

Theoretically AND gates with any number of inputs can be produced. The rule of operation is, however, the same—the output is a 1 only when all the inputs are 1.

OR gates

Schematic representation	Boolean algebra	Truth table
A, B inputs; C output	$C = A+B$	

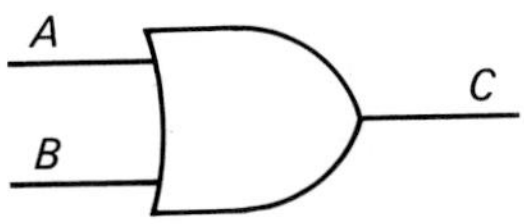

A	B	C
0	0	0
0	1	1
1	0	1
1	1	1

Fig. 1.11. A two input OR gate.

OR gates with several inputs can be produced. The rule of operation, however, is the same. The output is a 1 when any, some or all of the inputs are 1.

NOR gates

A NOR gate is a negated OR gate and could be represented by an OR gate followed by an INVERTER.

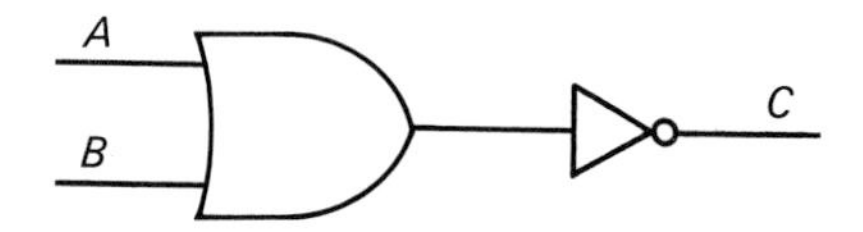

Fig. 1.12. A NOR gate circuit.

NOR gates are commonly used logic elements and the schematic representation is simplified to that shown in Fig. 1.13.

Schematic representation — Denotes inversion; inputs A, B; output C

Boolean algebra

$$C = \overline{A+B}$$

Truth table

A	B	C
0	0	1
0	1	0
1	0	0
1	1	0

Fig. 1.13. A two input NOR gate.

NOR gates with any number of inputs can be produced but the rule of operation is the same. The output is a 1 when all inputs are 0.

NAND gates

NAND gates can be produced in a similar way to NOR gates that is by connecting the output from an AND gate to the input of an INVERTER.

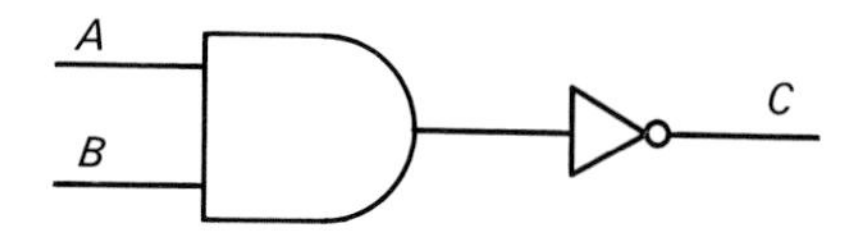

Fig. 1.14. A NAND gate circuit.

Again, since these are commonly used logic elements, the schematic representation is simplified to that shown in Fig. 1.15.

Schematic representation | **Boolean algebra** | **Truth table**

Denotes inversion

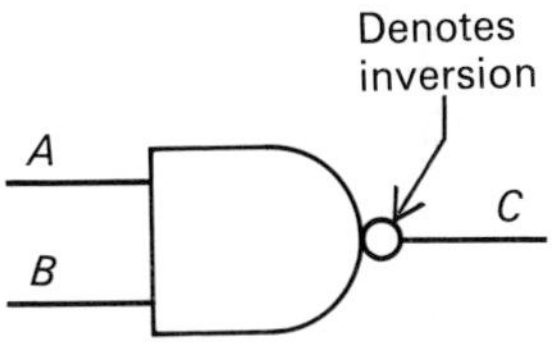

$C = \overline{A.B}$

A	B	C
0	0	1
0	1	1
1	0	1
1	1	0

Fig. 1.15. A two input NAND gate.

NAND gates with any number of inputs can be produced. The rule of operation is that the output is only an 0 when all the inputs are 1.

EXCLUSIVE OR gates

There is one other commonly produced logical gate, the two input EXCLUSIVE OR. The output from this gate is a 1 when either of the two inputs is a 1, but not when both are. In other words, the conditions when the output is equal to 1 exclude the case when both inputs are 1.

Schematic representation | **Boolean algebra** | **Truth table**

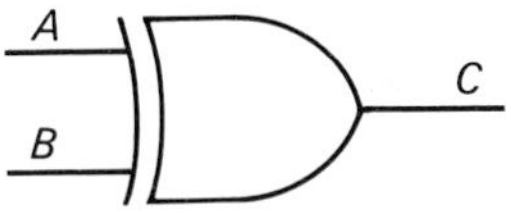

$C = A \oplus B$

A	B	C
0	0	0
0	1	1
1	0	1
1	1	0

Fig. 1.16. An EXCLUSIVE OR gate.

The combinational logic gates described above have all been implemented in TTL-integrated circuit chips. The packaging and electrical characteristics of these integrated circuits are described fully in Appendix 1.

Chapter 2

The Analysis and Design of Logic Circuits

2.1 INTRODUCTION

This chapter describes the methods used to develop Boolean expressions for a logical operation, the methods for simplifying these expressions, and for designing the logic circuit to perform the specified operation.

2.2 THE DIAGRAMMATIC REPRESENTATION OF LOGICAL FUNCTIONS

Logical expressions can be represented diagrammatically with the aid of Venn diagrams. A square is used to represent the universal class being considered. This class may be subdivided into a number of sub-classes as illustrated in Fig. 2.1.

Let the square represent the population of a country, and the circle that part of the population which is over 21 years of age.

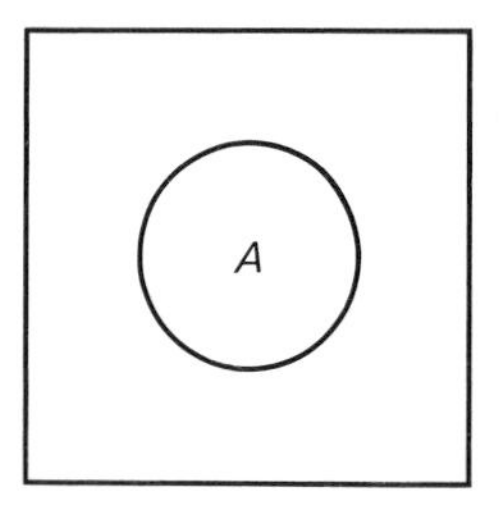

Fig. 2.1

The area outside the circle will then represent the part of the population which is not over 21 years of age.

In logic terms the area of the circle represents the class in which the variable $A = 1$ and the area outside it, the class in which $\bar{A} = 1$.

Consider a Venn diagram for a circuit with two inputs A and B, these are drawn as overlapping circles as shown in Fig. 2.2.

The shaded area then represents the case where A or B, or both A and B are 1, i.e. the logical function $A+B = 1$.

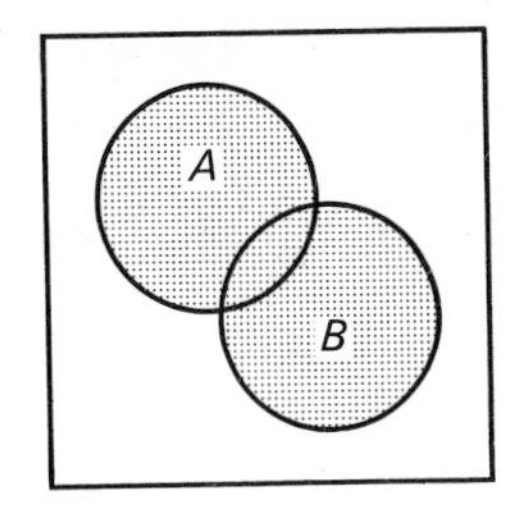

Fig. 2.2

Figure 2.3 shows the Venn diagrams for the logical functions AND, NAND and NOR.

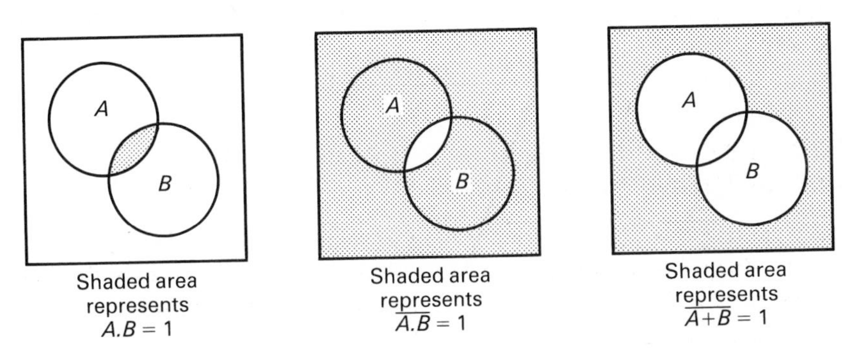

Fig. 2.3

From these diagrams simple logical relationships may be seen, for example:

$$\bar{A}+\bar{B}=\overline{A.B}$$
$$\bar{A}.\bar{B}=\overline{A+B}$$

These expressions are known as De Morgan's Law and represent the method of changing logical expressions in terms of OR to expressions in terms of AND and vice versa.

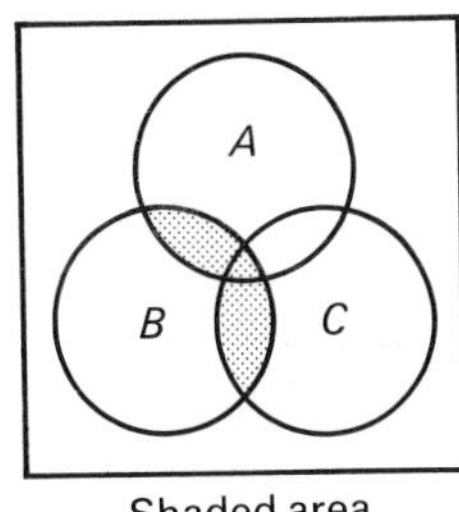

Shaded area represents $A.B + B.C = 1$

Fig. 2.4

Venn diagrams can be used to represent logical expressions with any number of variables. Figure 2.4 represents a logic circuit with three inputs and the shaded area the condition $A.B+B.C = 1$.

2.3 BOOLEAN ALGEBRA

In the expression $A.B+\bar{A}.C+D.(\bar{B}+\bar{C})+\bar{D}.E$ there are five variables $ABCD$ and E and nine literals being defined as the appearance of a variable or its complement. Boolean algebra expressions like the one above can be manipulated and simplified using the following laws.

Laws of Identity Agressivity and Neutrality of 0 and 1

(a) OR $A+0 = A$
$A+1 = 1$
(b) AND $A.0 = 0$
$A.1 = A$

Commutative Laws

(c) OR $A+B = B+A$
(d) AND $A.B = B.A$

Associative Laws

(e) OR $A+B+C = A+(B+C)$
$= (A+B)+C$
(f) AND $A.B.C = (A.B).C$
$= A.(B.C)$

Distributive Laws

(g) $A+(B.C) = (A+B).(A+C)$
(h) $A.(B+C) = (A.B)+(A.C)$

Laws of Absorption

(i) OR $A+A=A$
(j) $A+(A.B) = A$
(k) AND $A.A = A$
(l) $A.(A+B) = A$

Laws (j) and (l) can be illustrated using Venn diagrams as shown in Fig. 2.5, and also through the truth table shown in Table 2.1.

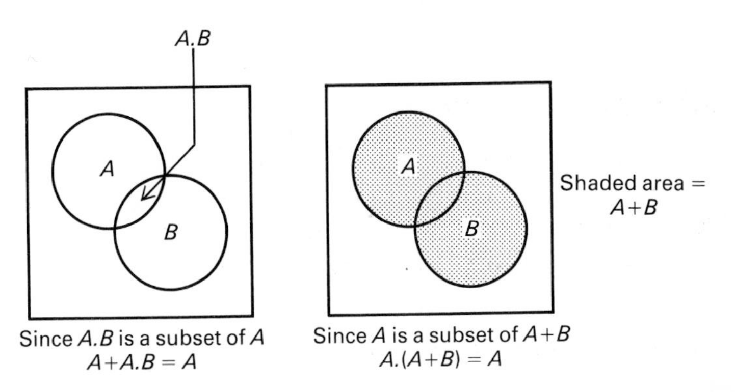

Fig. 2.5

Table 2.1

A	B	$A.B$	$A+(A.B)$	$A+B$	$A.(A+B)$
0	0	0	0	0	0
0	1	0	0	1	0
1	0	0	1	1	1
1	1	1	1	1	1

Laws of Absorption of Negation

(m) OR $A + (\bar{A}.B) = A + B$
(n) $\bar{A} + (A.B) = \bar{A} + B$
(o) AND $\bar{A}.(A + B) = \bar{A}.B$
(p) $A.(\bar{A} = B) = A.B$

Laws (m) and (o) can be proved using the truth table in Table 2.2. Laws (n) and (p) can be proved in a similar way.

Table 2.2

A	B	$\bar{A}$	$\bar{B}$	$\bar{A}.B$	$A+(\bar{A}.B)$	$A+B$	$\bar{A}.(A+B)$
0	0	1	1	0	0	0	0
0	1	1	0	1	1	1	1
1	0	0	1	0	1	1	0
1	1	0	0	0	1	1	0

Law of Double Negation

(q) $\bar{\bar{A}} = A$

Law of Excluded Middle

(r) $A + \bar{A} = 1$
(s) $A.\bar{A} = 0$

The Law of Excluded Middle is proved in the truth table below (Table 2.3).

Table 2.3

A	$\bar{A}$	$A + \bar{A}$	$A.\bar{A}$
0	1	1	0
1	0	1	0

Laws of Negation of Sums and Products (De Morgan's Laws)

(t) $\overline{A + B} = \bar{A}.\bar{B}$
(u) $\overline{A.B} = \bar{A} + \bar{B}$

These Laws are proved in the truth table below (Table 2.4).

Table 2.4

A	B	$A + B$	$\overline{A + B}$	$\bar{A}$	$\bar{B}$	$\bar{A}.\bar{B}$	$A.B$	$\overline{A.B}$	$\bar{A} + \bar{B}$
0	0	0	1	1	1	1	0	1	1
0	1	1	0	1	0	0	0	1	1
1	0	1	0	0	1	0	0	1	1
1	1	1	0	0	0	0	1	0	0

2.4 LOGIC DESIGN

The logic elements already described can be used as the basic building blocks in a logic system and it is now a matter of design to establish the particular configuration required.

The laws of Boolean algebra can be used to manipulate logical expressions into the required form for implementation as a digital circuit.

The following three simple examples illustrate this process. In each case the circuit has been designed using NAND gates and INVERTERS, since these are commonly available on integrated circuit chips.

Example 2.1

Using NAND gates and INVERTERS only, design a NOR gate truth table. The Boolean algebra expression for a NOR gate is

$$OP = \overline{A+B}$$

A	B	$A+B$
0	0	1
0	1	0
1	0	0
0	0	0

Truth table

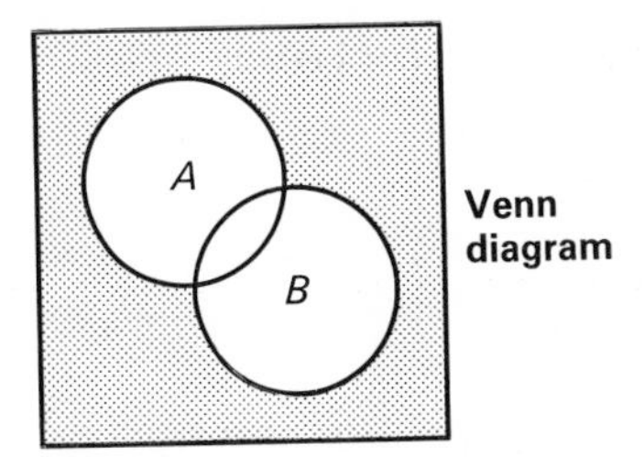

Fig. 2.6

By using De Morgan's Law the OR function can be converted to an AND

$$OP = \overline{A+B} = \bar{A}.\bar{B}$$

However the solution requires the use of NAND gates and INVERTERS only and to get a NAND function the OP must be inverted

$$\overline{OP} = \overline{\bar{A}.\bar{B}}$$

To get the required output rather than its inverse the Law of Double Negation is used

$$OP = \overline{\overline{OP}} = \overline{\overline{\bar{A}.\bar{B}}}$$

The circuit diagram can then be drawn as follows: Taking the term $\bar{A}$

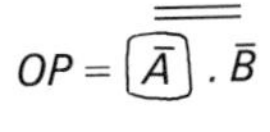

gives

$A \rightarrow$ [inverter] $\rightarrow \bar{A}$

Including the term $\bar{B}$

$$OP = \overline{\overline{\bar{A}.\bar{B}}}$$

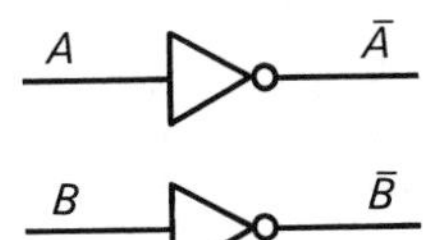

Including the NAND function

$$OP = \overline{\overline{\bar{A}.\bar{B}}}$$

yields

and finally including the inversion

$$OP = \overline{\overline{\bar{A}.\bar{B}}}$$

gives the circuit diagram as shown in Fig. 2.7.

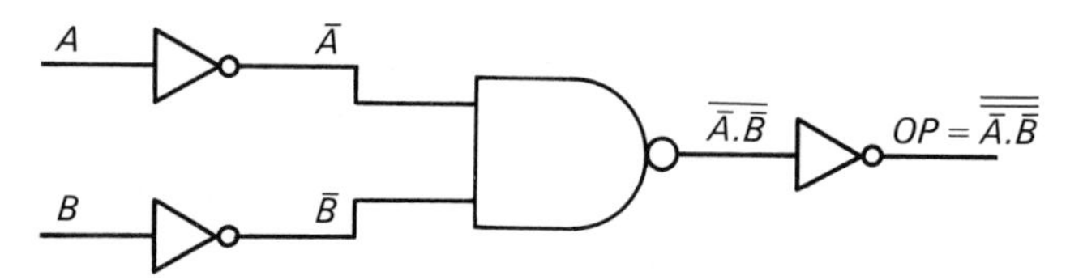

Fig. 2.7

Using an AND gate the circuit would be that shown in Fig. 2.8. or using a NOR gate directly, that in Fig. 2.9.

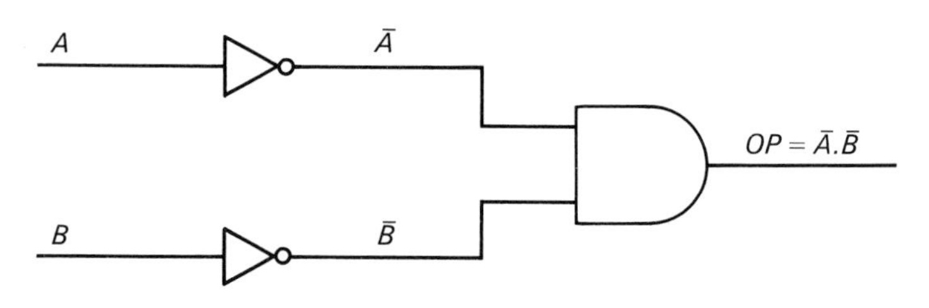

Fig. 2.8

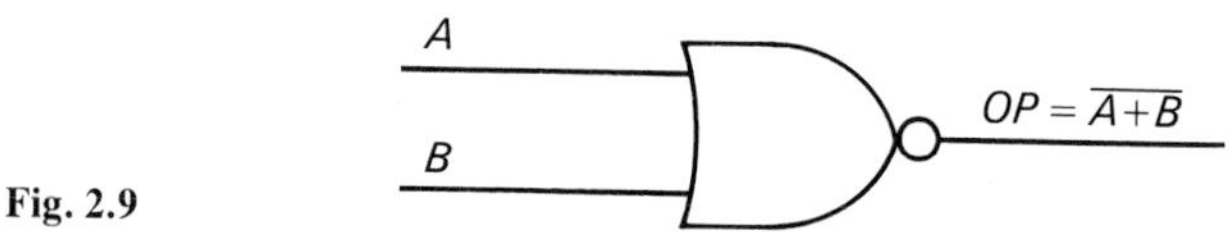

Fig. 2.9

Example 2.2

Using NAND gates and INVERTERS design an EXCLUSIVE OR gate.

The truth table and Venn diagram for an EXCLUSIVE OR gate are shown in Fig. 2.10. From the truth table it can be seen that the output is 1 when $\bar{A}$ *and* B are both 1 *or* when A *and* $\bar{B}$ are both 1. Written in Boolean algebra this gives the expression

$$OP = \bar{A}B + A\bar{B}$$

Truth table

A	B	OP
0	0	0
0	1	1
1	0	1
1	1	0

Venn diagram

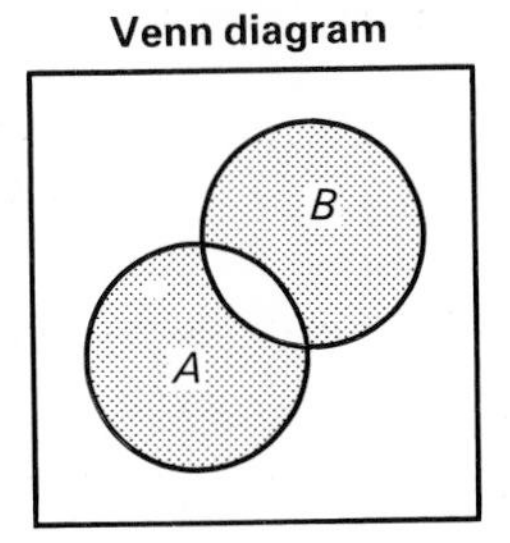

Fig. 2.10

The solution asks for NAND gates and INVERTERS only. To convert the OR function to AND the expression must first be inverted and then De Morgan's Law used:

$$\overline{OP} = \overline{\bar{A}B + A\bar{B}}$$

$$\overline{OP} = \overline{\bar{A}B}.\overline{A\bar{B}}$$

The resulting expression for $\overline{OP}$ must then be negated to give the required output

$$OP = \overline{\overline{OP}} = \overline{\overline{\bar{A}B}.\overline{A\bar{B}}}$$

This function then leads directly to the circuit diagram given in Fig. 2.11.

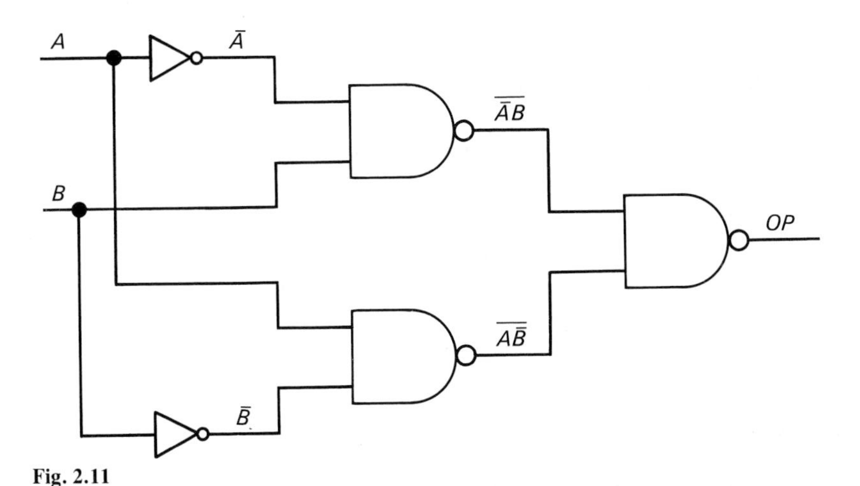

Fig. 2.11

Example 2.3

Using NAND gates and INVERTERS only design a simplified circuit for the function expressed in the following truth table shown in Fig. 2.12.

Inputs			Output
A	*B*	*C*	*D*
0	0	0	0
0	0	1	0
0	1	0	0
0	1	1	1
1	0	0	0
1	0	1	0
1	1	0	1
1	1	1	1

Fig. 2.12

From the truth table the Boolean expression obtained is

$$D = \overline{AB}C + AB\bar{C} + ABC.$$

To aid simplification the term ABC is duplicated:
Law of Absorption

$$D = \bar{A}BC + ABC + AB\bar{C} + ABC,$$

which gives, using the Distributive Law,

$$D = (\bar{A} + A)BC + AB(\bar{C} + C)$$

Using the Law of Excluded Middle,

$$D = BC.1 + AB.1,$$

and the Law of Agressivity or Neutrality of 0 or 1 gives

$$D = BC + AB$$

The required function has then to be converted to AND using negation and De Morgan's Law.

$$\bar{D} = \overline{BC + AB}$$

$$\bar{D} = \overline{BC}.\overline{AB}$$

and the required output obtained using the Law of Double Negation

$$D = \bar{\bar{D}} \quad \overline{\overline{BC}.\overline{AB}}$$

This expression gives the circuit diagram in Fig. 2.13.

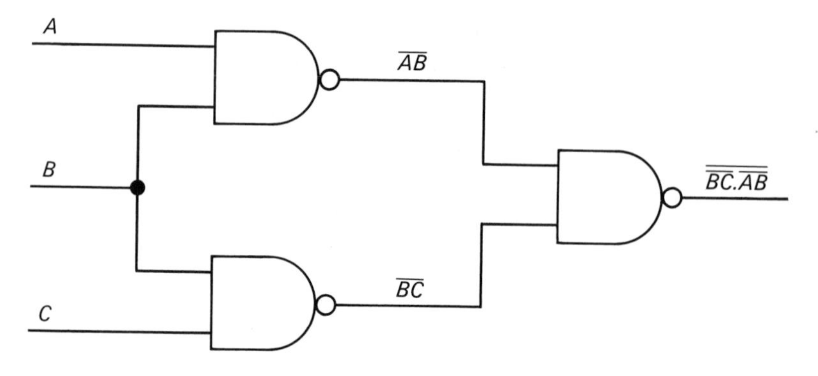

Fig. 2.13

From the previous example it can be seen that synthesis of circuits using Boolean algebra can be fairly involved and difficult. A more straightforward approach is to use Karnaugh maps, which are a graphical method of synthesizing digital circuits based on Venn diagrams.

2.5 KARNAUGH MAPS

Drawing a map

To draw a Karnaugh map a square is constructed and subdivided for each of the possible combinations of inputs. The squares are then coded. For a circuit with two inputs the four possible combinations of inputs are represented as shown in Fig. 2.14. Note that the Boolean algebra for each input condition is *not* written in the squares when synthesizing a circuit but has been included in Figs 2.14, 2.16 and 2.17 for clarification.

B \ A	0	1
0	$\bar{A}\bar{B}$	$A\bar{B}$
1	$\bar{A}B$	AB

Inputs A	Inputs B	Boolean
0	0	$\bar{A}\bar{B}$
0	1	$\bar{A}B$
1	0	$A\bar{B}$
1	1	AB

Fig. 2.14

The squares are usually coded in reflected binary (Gray Code) notation for both the columns and rows to ensure that adjacent squares have a change in only one variable.

Decimal	Bit No. 3	2	1	0	
0	0	0	0	0	
1	0	0	0	1	
					Reflect
2	0	0	1	1	
3	0	0	1	0	
					Reflect
4	0	1	1	0	
5	0	1	1	1	
6	0	1	0	1	
7	0	1	0	0	
					Reflect
8	1	1	0	0	
9	1	1	0	1	
					etc.

Fig. 2.15

Thus the Karnaugh map for three inputs case is that shown in Fig. 2.16, and that for four inputs is shown in Fig. 2.17.

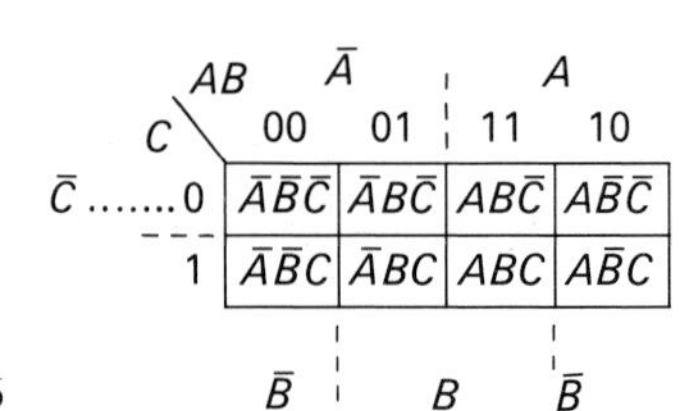

Fig. 2.16

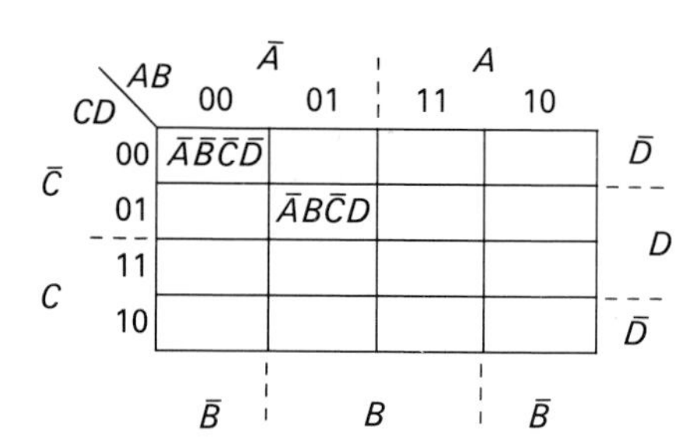

Fig. 2.17

The Karnaugh map is then completed by writing the output condition in each box. The Karnaugh map for the function expressed in the truth table (Table 2.5), is given in Fig. 2.18.

Table 2.5

A	*B*	*C*	*OP*
0	0	0	0
0	0	1	0
0	1	0	0
0	1	1	1
1	0	0	0
1	0	1	1
1	1	0	0
1	1	1	1

	C \ AB	00	01	11	10
$\bar{C}$	0	0	0	0	0
C	1	0	1	1	1

(A above 00 01; A above 11 10; $\bar{B}$ B $\bar{B}$ below)

Fig. 2.18

The method of simplification

Pairs of adjacent outputs

Only one input variable changes between adjacent positions on the Karnaugh map. If an adjacent pair of inputs have outputs of 1 the Boolean expression for them is independent of one of the input variables.

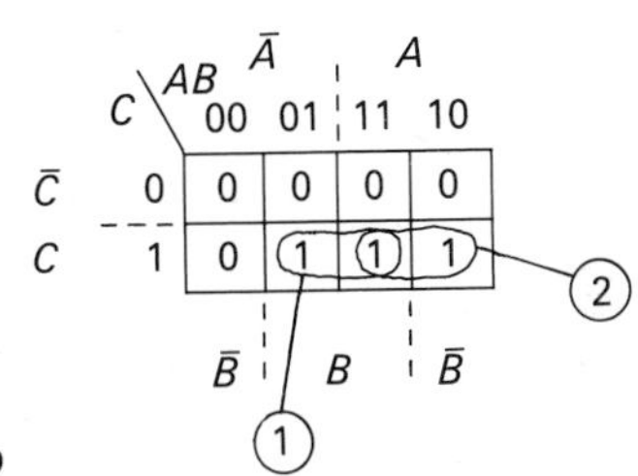

Fig. 2.19

In the example given in Table 2.5 above there are two pairs of adjacent outputs, see Fig. 2.19. Taking pair (1), these outputs are independent of A and hence the expression for this pair is

$$OP = BC \quad (1)$$

The remaining input conditions for which the OP is 1 is $A\bar{B}C$ and the overall expression could be

$$OP = BC + A\bar{B}C$$

However, the second pair (2) can be included, these outputs are independant of B and for this pair the output would be given by

$$OP = AC \quad (2)$$

Hence the simplification for the circuit can be obtained by combining equations (1) and (2) giving

$$OP = BC + AC \quad (3)$$

This same expression can also be obtained using Boolean algebra:
From the truth table (Table 2.5),

$$OP = \bar{A}BC + A\bar{B}C + ABC$$

Adding an additional ABC,

$$OP = \bar{A}BC + ABC + A\bar{B}C + ABC$$

By the Distributive Law,

$$OP = BC(\bar{A} + A) + AC(\bar{B} + B)$$

By the Law of Excluded Middle

$$OP = BC.1 + AC.1,$$

and by the Law of Agressivity and Neutrality of 0 and 1

$$OP = BC + AC$$

This leads to the circuit diagram shown in Fig. 2.20.

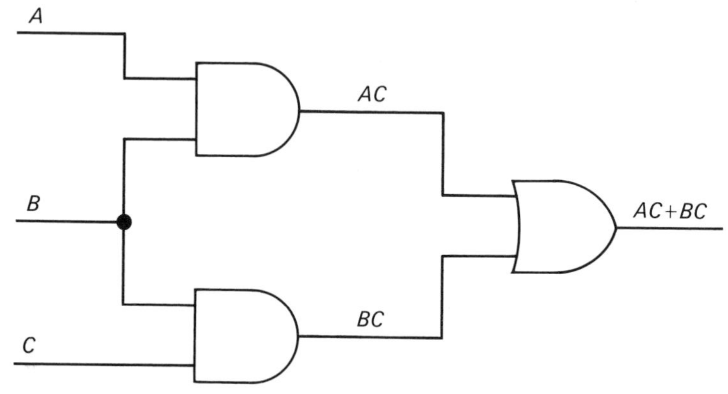

Fig. 2.20

If the circuit had to use NAND gates and INVERTERS only:

$$\overline{OP} = \overline{BC + AC},$$

which by De Morgan's Law gives

$$\overline{OP} = \overline{BC}.\overline{AC}$$

and by the Law of Double Negation

$$OP = \overline{\overline{OP}} \quad \overline{\overline{BC}.\overline{AC}}$$

which gives an alternative circuit diagram shown in Fig. 2.21.

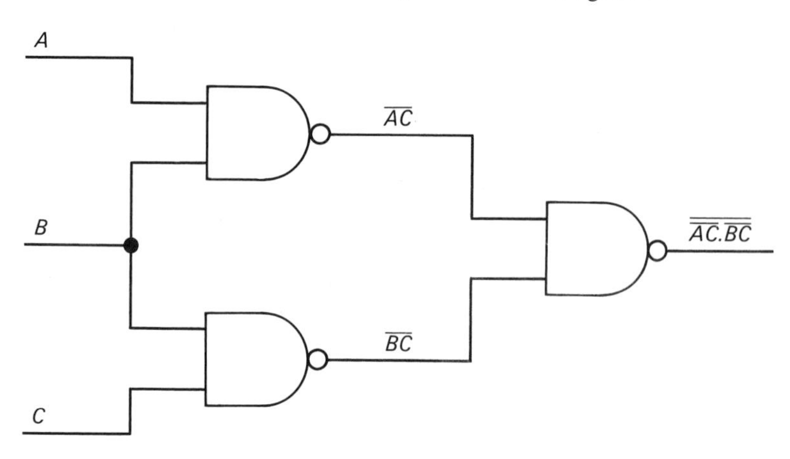

Fig. 2.21

Groups of four adjacent outputs

In a similar way to the reduction due to adjacent pairs, a group of four input conditions which give an output of 1, whether in a straight line or a square, imply that the expression for the output is independent of two of the inputs.

Consider the function shown in Table 2.6, the Karnaugh map is shown in Fig. 2.22.

Table 2.6

A	B	C	OP
0	0	0	0
0	0	1	0
0	1	0	1
0	1	1	1
1	0	0	0
1	0	1	0
1	1	0	1
1	1	1	1

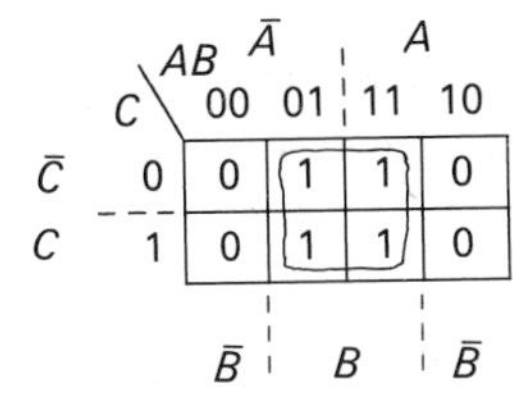

Fig. 2.22

The group of four input conditions for which the output is a 1 is independant of both A and C and thus $OP = B$, which can be quite easily confirmed from the truth table.

Spherical characteristics

The maps are spherical rather like a map of the world, and hence the left and right edges are adjacent as are the top and bottom of the map. The following two cases illustrate the conditions which can arise:

Consider the function specified in the truth table shown in Table 2.7. The Karnaugh map is that in Fig. 2.23. From pair (1), $OP_1 = BC$, the pair of input conditions labelled (2) are adjacent and hence

$$OP_1 = \bar{B}C$$

The overall expression for the output is therefore

$$OP = B\bar{C} + \bar{B}C,$$

and the circuit diagram is as shown in Fig. 2.24.

Table 2.7

A	B	C	OP
0	0	0	0
0	0	1	1
0	1	0	1
0	1	1	0
1	0	0	0
1	0	1	1
1	1	0	1
1	1	1	0

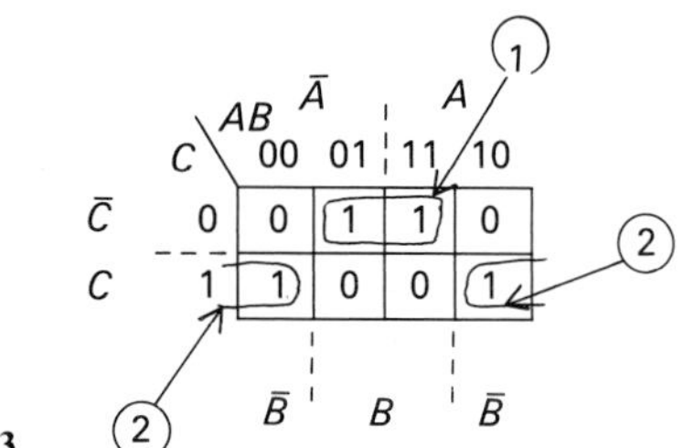

Fig. 2.23

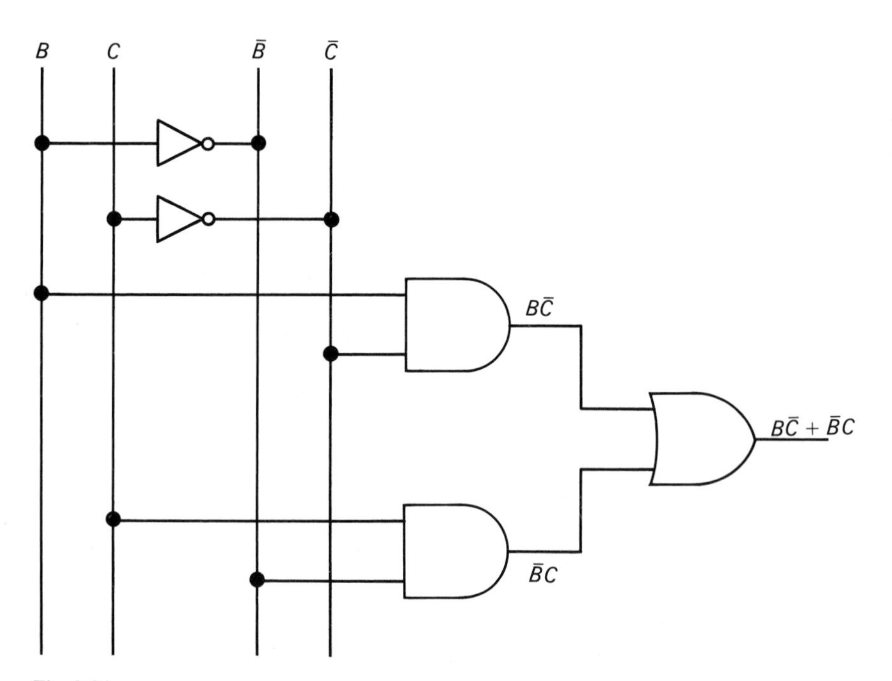

Fig. 2.24

The example below is of a four input system and makes use of the spherical characteristic of all four corners being adjacent.

Example 2.4

Using NAND gates and INVERTERS only, construct a circuit diagram for the function given in the truth table in Table 2.8. The Karnaugh map for the function is shown in Fig. 2.25.

Table 2.8

A	B	C	D	OP
0	0	0	0	1
0	0	0	1	1
0	0	1	0	1
0	0	1	1	0
0	1	0	0	0
0	1	0	1	0
0	1	1	0	0
0	1	1	1	0
1	0	0	0	1
1	0	0	1	1
1	0	1	0	1
1	0	1	1	0
1	1	0	0	0
1	1	0	1	0
1	1	1	0	0
1	1	1	1	0

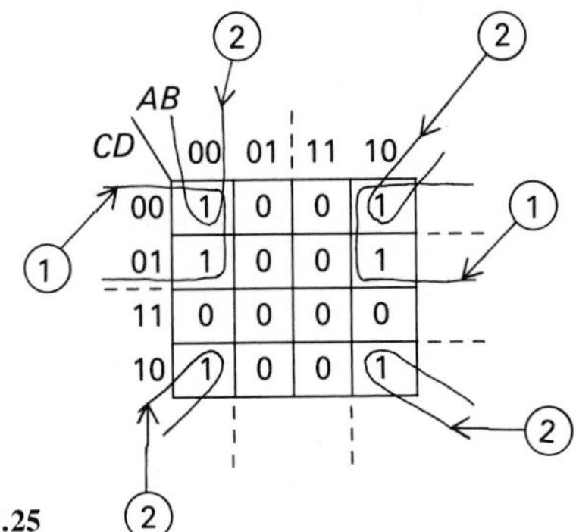

Fig. 2.25

Taking the group of four input conditions labelled (1). The output is independent of A and D and thus,

$$OP_1 = \bar{B}\bar{C}$$

Taking the four corners, the output is independent of A and C and thus

$$OP_2 = \bar{B}\bar{D}.$$

The overall Boolean expression is therefore

$$OP = \bar{B}\bar{C} + \bar{B}\bar{D}.$$

This must then be converted to an AND function

$$\overline{OP} = \overline{\bar{B}\bar{C} + \bar{B}\bar{D}}$$

and by De Morgan's Law

$$\overline{OP} = \overline{\bar{B}\bar{C}}.\overline{\bar{B}\bar{D}}$$

by the Law of Double Negation

$$OP = \overline{\overline{OP}} = \overline{\overline{\bar{B}\bar{C}}.\overline{\bar{B}\bar{D}}}$$

and the circuit diagram is shown in Fig. 2.26.

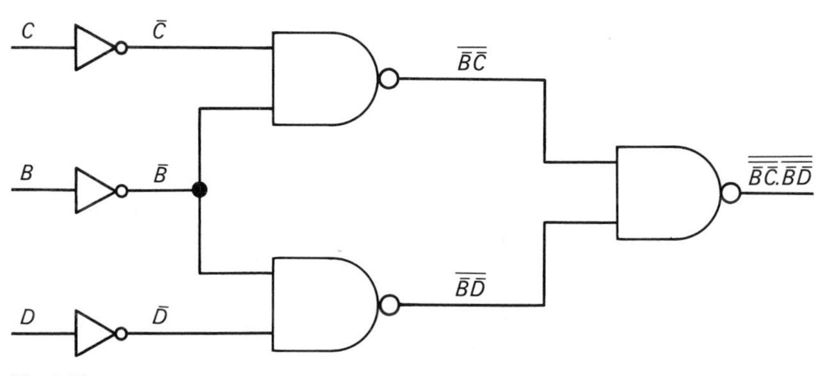

Fig. 2.26

Example 2.5

Using Karnaugh maps obtain the Boolean expression for the function given in the following truth table (Table 2.9), and using NAND gates and INVERTERS only, construct a circuit diagram. The Karnaugh map for this function is shown in Fig. 2.27.

Taking the group of four outputs labelled (1) in Fig. 2.27, the output is independent of B and C, i.e.

$$OP_1 = \overline{AD}$$

Taking the group of four input conditions labelled (2), the output is given by

$$OP_2 = BD$$

Taking the group of four labelled (3), the output is independent of B and C,

$$OP_3 = AD$$

Finally the pair labelled (4) are independent of D and thus

$$OP_4 = A\bar{B}\bar{C}$$

The overall Boolean expression is

$$OP = \overline{AD} + BD + AD + A\bar{B}\bar{C}$$

Table 2.9

A	B	C	D	OP
0	0	0	0	1
0	0	0	1	0
0	0	1	0	1
0	0	1	1	0
0	1	0	0	1
0	1	0	1	1
0	1	1	0	1
0	1	1	1	1
1	0	0	0	1
1	0	0	1	1
1	0	1	0	0
1	0	1	1	1
1	1	0	0	0
1	1	0	1	1
1	1	1	0	0
1	1	1	1	1

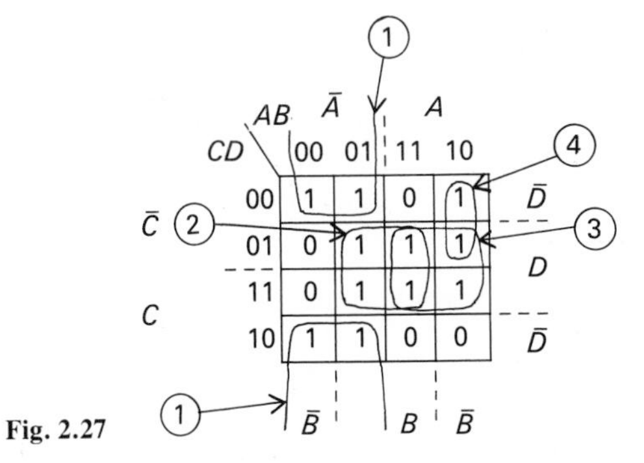

Fig. 2.27

An alternative expression may be obtained by considering the output = 0 conditions as shown in Fig. 2.28. This may well lead to a simpler circuit as there are fewer of zero outputs than ones.

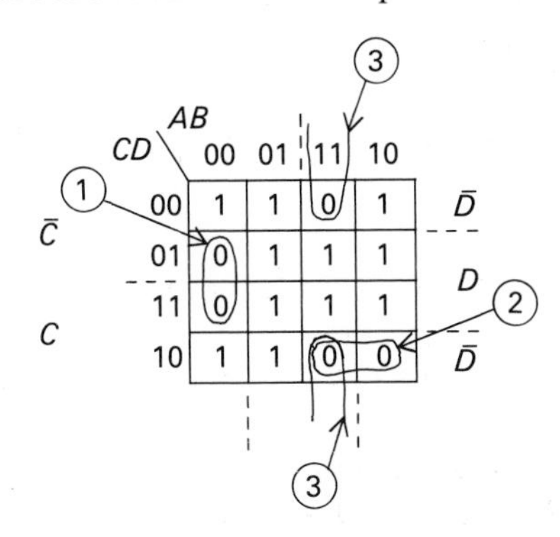

Fig. 2.28

Taking the outputs labelled (1), which are independent of C,

$$\overline{OP}_1 = \bar{A}\bar{B}D.$$

Taking the pair labelled (2),

$$\overline{OP}_2 = AC\bar{D}.$$

The pair (3) are independent of C,

$$\overline{OP}_3 = AB\bar{D},$$

and the overall expression is

$$\overline{OP} = \bar{A}\bar{B}D + AC\bar{D} + AB\bar{D}$$

This expression can then be converted to be in terms of NAND gates and INVERTERS only:

By the Law of Double Negation,

$$OP = \overline{\overline{OP}} = \overline{\bar{A}\bar{B}D + AC\bar{D} + AB\bar{D}}$$

using De Morgan's Law,

$$OP = \overline{\bar{A}\bar{B}D}.\overline{AC\bar{D}}.\overline{AB\bar{D}},$$

to get the overall expression in terms of NAND

$$\overline{OP} = \overline{\overline{\bar{A}\bar{B}D}.\overline{AC\bar{D}}.\overline{AB\bar{D}}}$$

and

$$OP = \overline{\overline{OP}} = \overline{\overline{\overline{\bar{A}\bar{B}D}.\overline{AC\bar{D}}.\overline{AB\bar{D}}}}.$$

The circuit diagram for this function is shown in Fig. 2.29.

Summary of the rules for the combination of input conditions using Karnaugh maps (cf. Fig. 2.29)

Rule 1

Every cell containing the required output condition must be included.

Rule 2

The largest possible cell groups must be formed (in powers of two only). Groups formed of 2^n cells eliminate n variables.

Rule 3

The required output condition must be contained in the minimum number of groups to avoid duplication.

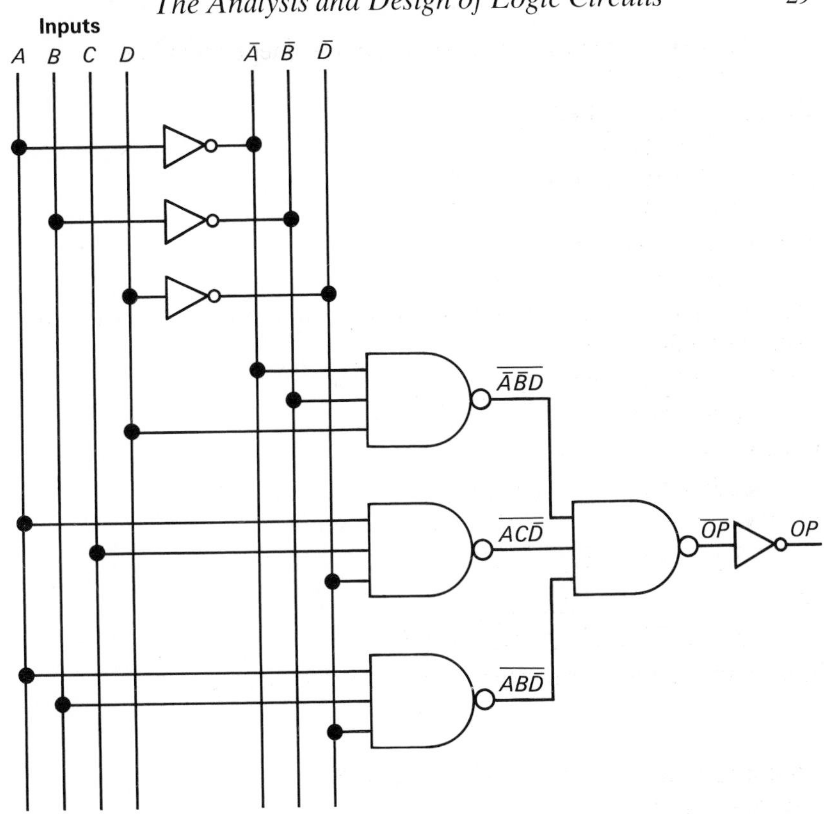
Inputs
A B C D
$\bar{A}$ $\bar{B}$ $\bar{D}$
$\overline{\bar{A}\bar{B}D}$
$\overline{AC\bar{D}}$
$\overline{AB\bar{D}}$
$\overline{OP}$
OP

Fig. 2.29

Chapter 3

The Representation of Data

3.1 INTRODUCTION

In the previous two chapters the basic concepts of combinational circuit design were introduced. This chapter describes the general configuration of a computer system and the ways in which data is stored.

The material introduced in this chapter will enable later chapters to expand on these techniques and to apply them to circuit designs which form some of the basic components of a digital computer.

3.2 THE BASIC COMPONENTS OF A COMPUTER SYSTEM

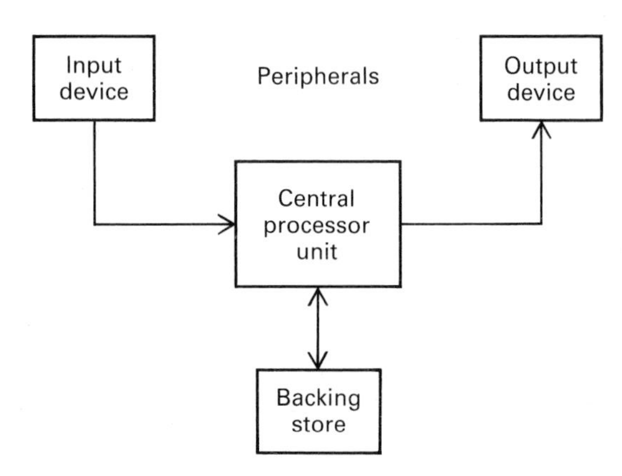

Fig. 3.1. Basic computer system components.

Any computer system has three basic components:

(i) Input and output devices or peripherals which are used for communication between the computer system and the outside world. A printer is an example of an output device and a visual display unit is an input/output peripheral, the keyboard being an input device and the screen an output device.

(ii) A central processing unit (CPU) into which programs are loaded and in which they are executed.

(iii) A backing store which is used to store programs and data from the CPU and from which either programs or data, or both, can rapidly be loaded into the CPU. A floppy disc is an example of a backing store.

3.3 THE CENTRAL PROCESSING UNIT

The central processing unit consists of:

(i) A set of registers, an arithmetic unit, and a control unit which together enable the CPU to execute instructions.

(ii) Memory in which both program instructions and data are stored.

(iii) Input output ports used to drive peripherals.

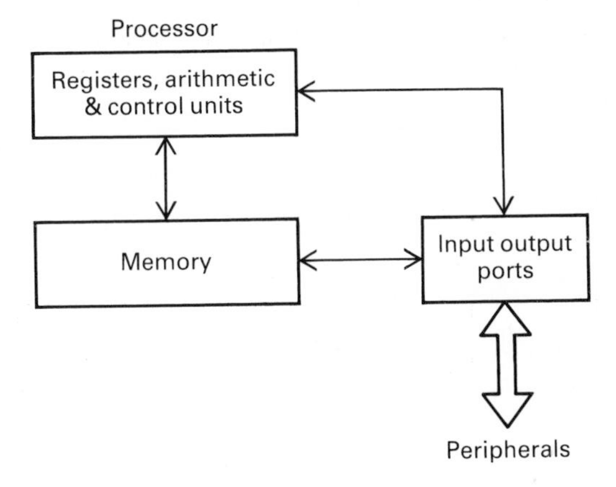

Fig. 3.2. The central processing unit.

The set of registers, the arithmetic unit and the control unit are often referred to as 'the processor' and connections between it and both the input/output ports and the memory are known as buses or highways.

3.4 MEMORY

All data and instructions are stored in binary format. The memory is organized as a large number of cells each of which has its own address, a positive integer unique to that cell. The size of the cell, known as a word, can vary from computer to computer as can the number of words in the main memory.

In general, words are usually between 8 and 64 bits long and are made up of bytes, a group of 8 bits which is the smallest addressable unit on a computer, and which can store one character. A group of 4 bits is sometimes referred to as a nibble and therefore a byte consists of 2 nibbles. Figure 3.3 shows the layout of a typical memory with 16-bit words.

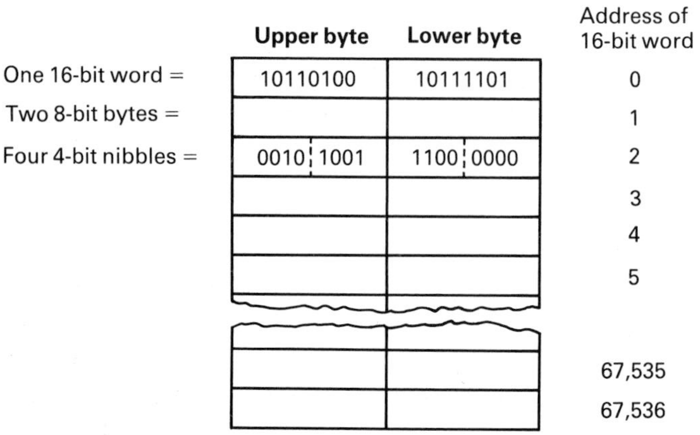

	Upper byte	Lower byte	Address of 16-bit word
One 16-bit word =	10110100	10111101	0
Two 8-bit bytes =			1
Four 4-bit nibbles =	0010 ¦ 1001	1100 ¦ 0000	2
			3
			4
			5
			67,535
			67,536

Fig. 3.3. 16-bit memory.

3.5 INTEGER NUMBERS

Each word or byte of memory holds either one instruction or one item of data. The simplest form of data that can be stored is an integer or whole number.

Decimal integers

Normal hand calculations are performed using a decimal system of numbers, a system in which the digits are to the base 10 and therefore with ten different characters (0 to 9) representing the value of each digit (cf. Fig. 3.4). The number 237 in decimal is two hundreds + three tens + seven units, or ($2\times10^2 + 3\times10^1 + 7\times10^0$) as each digit to the left increases in value by a factor of 10.

Digits	Thousands	Hundreds	Tens	Units
Powers of ten	10^3	10^2	10^1	10^0
Characters	0 to 9	0 to 9	0 to 9	0 to 9

Fig. 3.4. Decimal integers.

Binary integers

A similar technique is used in any numbering system. In binary the values of the digits increase by a factor of 2 for each position to the left and there are two different characters (0 and 1) representing each digit (cf. Fig. 3.5). The binary number 1101 is therefore, one eight + one four + zero twos + one unit (or $1 \times 2^3 + 1 \times 2^2 + 0 \times 2^1 + 1 \times 2^0$), i.e. 13_{10}.

Digits	Eights	Fours	Twos	Units
Power of two	2^3	2^2	2^1	2^0
Characters	0 to 1	0 to 1	0 to 1	0 to 1

Fig. 3.5. Binary integers.

Octal and hexadecimal

Two further numbering systems are widely used in computing, namely octal and hexadecimal, which are to the base 8 and the base 16_{10} respectively. Figure 3.6 below summarizes octal, and Fig. 3.7, hexadecimal. It should be noted that in hexadecimal 16_{10} characters are needed for each digit and so the characters *A*, *B*, *C*, *D*, *E* and *F* are used for the values 10_{10} to 15_{10} respectively.

Digits	Sixty-fours	Eights	Units
Powers of eight	8^2	8^1	8^0
Characters	0 to 7	0 to 7	0 to 7

Fig. 3.6. Octal integers.

Digits	Two hundred and sixty-fives	Sixteens	Units
Powers of sixteen	16^2	16^1	16^0
Characters	0 to 9 and A to F	0 to 9 and A to F	0 to 9 and A to F

Fig. 3.7. Hexadecimal integers.

Octal and hexadecimal are important in computing since they provide a shorthand way of representing three and four binary digits respectively as shown in Fig. 3.8.

Both octal and hexadecimal can be used as a shorthand representation for binary. For example the 12-bit binary number 011101101111_2 can be represented in octal and hexadecimal as

$$011\ 101\ 101\ 111 = 3557_8$$
$$0111\ 0110\ 1111 = 76F_{16}.$$

Decimal	Binary	Octal	Hexadecimal
0	0000	0	0
1	0001	1	1
2	0010	2	2
3	0011	3	3
4	0100	4	4
5	0101	5	5
6	0110	6	6
7	0111	7	7
8	1000	10	8
9	1001	11	9
10	1010	12	A
11	1011	13	B
12	1100	14	C
13	1101	15	D
14	1110	16	E
15	1111	17	F

Fig. 3.8. Octal and hexadecimal as a shorthand for binary.

Storage of integers

The format used to store any data in a computer system depends only on the interpretation of the binary pattern made by the hardware and software.

Integers are usually stored in computer words in a binary format with the most significant bit representing the sign of the number, a 0 indicating a positive integer and a 1 a negative integer.

An 8-bit byte can therefore store positive integers in the range 00000000_2 to 01111111, i.e. 0_{10} to 127_{10}.

The convention usually adopted for storing negative integers is known as 'two's complement'. This convention is widely used since it allows arithmetic operations to be performed without any corrections having to be made on the binary pattern for the result. To obtain the two's complement of a binary number each bit of the number is inverted and 1 added.

Take the number 11_{10} held in 8 bits:

$$
\begin{array}{lcr}
11_{10} & = & 00001011 \\
\text{Invert} & = & 11110100 \\
\text{Add 1} & & +\ 1 \\
\hline
-11_{10} & & 11110101
\end{array}
$$

Note that the most significant bit is a 1 indicating a negative number. The range of negative numbers that can be stored in 8 bits is 11111111 to 10000000, i.e. -1_{10} to -128_{10}.

3.6 FRACTIONS

Decimal fractions are represented in the form 0.124_{10} with the digits to the right of the decimal point representing a decrease in the powers of ten for each place moved (cf. Fig. 3.9).

Digit		Tenths	Hundredths	Thousandths
	Decimal			
Powers of ten	point	10^{-1}	10^{-2}	10^{-3}
Characters		0 to 9	0 to 9	0 to 9

Fig. 3.9. Decimal fractions.

In a similar way a bit pattern can be interpreted as being a binary fraction with the value of each bit reducing by a power of two for each place moved to the right. For example, $0.1101_2 = (0.5 + 0.25 + 0.0625_{10})$. Figure 3.10 summarizes the convention.

Digit		Halves	Quarters	Eigths
	Binary			
Powers of two	point	2^{-1}	2^{-2}	2^{-3}
Digits		0 and 1	0 and 1	0 and 1

Fig. 3.10. Binary fractions.

The convention used to interpret a bit pattern as a binary fraction is the same as that used for integers, namely two's complement form but with an *assumed* binary point between the sign bit and the most significant data dit. Thus the binary pattern 01000000 can be interpreted as being 0.5_{10} as well as 64_{10} and it is the programmer, when writing the program, who specifies the interpretation of the pattern. Similarly 10100000 can represent -0.75_{10} or -96_{10}.

3.7 FLOATING POINT NUMBERS

It can be seen from Section 3.5 that by adopting a two's complement notation for a computer with an n-bit word integer, numbers in the range 2^{n-1} to -2^n can be stored.

In almost all mathematical calculations real numbers are used, e.g. 427.16_{10} and it is essential that this type of number can be handled on a digital computer.

In decimal the real number can be normalized, i.e. converted into a form consisting of the largest possible fraction raised to an integer power of ten,

$$427.16_{10} = 0.42716 \times 10^3$$
$$0.01642 = 0.1642 \times 10^{-1}$$

The fractional part is known as the mantissa and the integer part as the exponent.

In a digital computer a binary floating point number is stored as a binary fraction raised to an integer power of two (cf. Fig. 3.11).

Binary $0{\cdot}10010000 \times 10^{0100}$
Assumed binary point
Decimal $0{\cdot}5625 \times 2^4 = 4{\cdot}5_{10}$

Fig. 3.11. Floating point number.

In practice only the fractional mantissa and the integer exponent are stored, the exact format depending on the word length of the computer and the conventions adopted.

Instructions to perform the addition and subtraction of integer numbers form part of the instruction sets of all machines. Some of the larger microcomputers, minicomputers and mainframes include integer multiply and divide instructions and may have special purpose hardware for floating point operations.

3.8 CHARACTERS

In addition to holding numeric information many of the applications of computers require the capture, storage and retrieval of text. A number of formats for the transmission and storage of characters have been developed but the two most widely adopted are the 8-bit Extended Binary Coded Decimal Interchange Code or EBCDIC, originated by IBM, and the 7-bit American Standard Code for Information Interchange or ASCII. Only ASCII will be described below but both character sets are specified in Appendix 4.

Each ASCII character is stored using 7 data bits, giving an 128 character set. This set is split up into seven groups of 16 characters, bits 0 to 3 giving the character and bits 4 to 6 the group or zone. The eighth and most significant bit is called the parity bit and is used (if required) to check that the character has been read correctly. The parity bit is used to ensure that each character is represented by a pattern with an even number of 1's, even parity, or alternatively, by a pattern with an odd number of 1's—odd parity, the type of parity used depending on the convention chosen for the particular computer system.

The characters *A* to *O* have zone identification of 4 and are represented by the numeric values 1 to 15 respectively. Thus the character *E* in even parity ASCII will be:

1	100	0101
Parity = 1 to give four 1's in the pattern	Zone identification	Numeric identification

The numeric characters 0 to 9 have a zone representation of 3 and a numeric representation of 0 to 9 respectively. Thus the character 6_{10} is even parity ASCII will be:

0	011	0110
Parity = 0 to give an even number of 1's	Zone identification	Numeric identification

3.9 BINARY CODED DECIMAL

Numeric data is input in decimal and transmitted in a form where the least significant 4 bits represent the value of the decimal digit.

If only relatively simple and few arithmetic operations are to be performed on this data it may be stored using only the (Binary Coded Decimal or BCD) 4 least significant bits to represent each decimal digit and special instructions may exist to enable addition and subtraction of numbers held in this form. For example 4219_{10} would be held in BCD as:

0100 0010 0001 1001

in 2 bytes.

Once again it must be stressed that all data and instructions within a computer system are stored simply as a binary pattern, the interpretation of that pattern as an integer, fraction, character, BCD number, or even as a machine code instruction is defined by the software and is at the discretion of the programmer.

Chapter 4

The Arithmetic and Logic Unit

4.1 INTRODUCTION

The arithmetic and logic unit is one of the main functional units within a digital computer and as its name implies it is where both arithmetic and logical operations are performed.

The chapter starts by explaining how binary addition is performed and then shows how simple logic gates can be used to implement this in hardware. A similar approach is followed to introduce the techniques used in subtraction and the two circuits are combined together with a control signal to produce an adder/subtractor unit.

As well as performing addition and subtraction, an arithmetic unit will also be capable of performing comparisons on binary data to enable conditional operations to be carried out. Various types of comparator are discussed and their implementation in hardware explained.

Finally, the concept of shifting is introduced and a simple arithmetic and logic unit described.

4.2 BINARY ADDITION

The simplest arithmetic operation that can be performed is the addition of two single-bit binary numbers. Only four possible combinations can occur and these are shown in Fig. 4.1.

	(i)	(ii)	(iii)	(iv)
A_0	0	0	1	1
B_0	+0	+1	+0	+1
Sum S_0	0	1	1	1 0

(In case (iv), the leading 1 is marked: carry to next stage)

Fig. 4.1. Single-bit binary addition.

The first three cases are straightforward, however, in case (iv) it must be remembered that the addition is being performed in binary and not decimal. This means that the answer, 2_{10} (decimal) is equivalent to a *sum* (S_0) of 0 with a 1 carried to the next most significant position. This carry bit is given the label C_0 (the carry out of the bit 0 position).

The half-adder

These four additions can be summarized in a truth table (cf. Table 4.1) having two inputs (A_0, B_0) and two outputs (S_0, C_0).

In the first three cases no carry is produced and a 0 is entered in the appropriate column.

Table 4.1

	A_0	B_0	S_0	C_0
(i)	0	0	0	0
(ii)	0	1	1	0
(iii)	1	0	1	0
(iv)	1	1	0	1

The truth table in Table 4.1 specifies the operation of a binary logic circuit which can be designed using the techniques introduced in Chapter 1, thus

$$S_0(sum) = \bar{A}_0.B_0 + A_0.\bar{B}_0$$
$$C.(carry) = A_0.B_0$$

Using AND, OR and INVERTER gates these equations can be implemented with the logic circuit shown in Fig. 4.2. This circuit is known

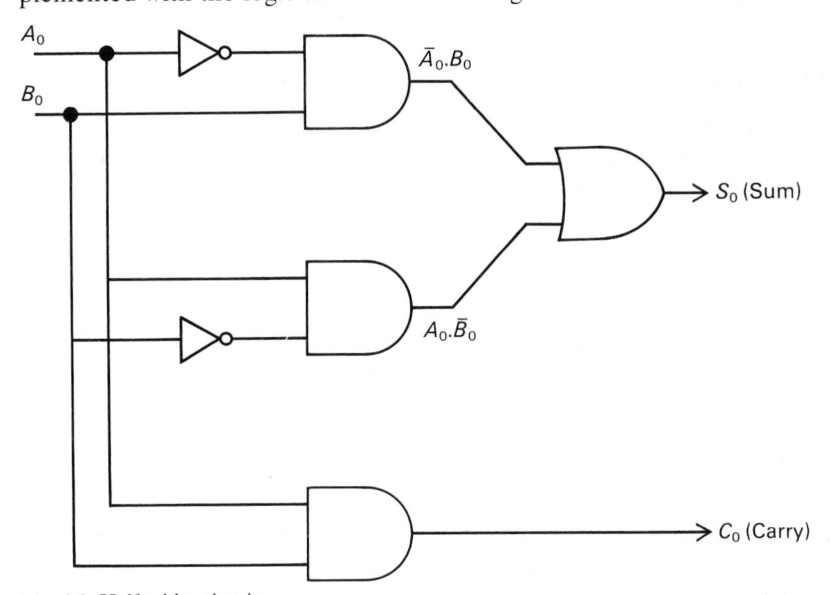

Fig. 4.2. Half-adder circuit.

as a binary *half-adder*, and forms a fundamental building block within the arithmetic unit of a computer.

For most logical functions it is possible to design several different logic circuits which will meet the requirements specified in the truth table. One alternative implementation for the half-adder is shown in Fig. 4.3. This was designed by noticing that the pattern in the S column of the truth table is in fact identical to that produced by an EXCLUSIVE OR gate. This gate was then used to replace two AND gates, two INVERTERS and the OR gate used in Fig. 4.2.

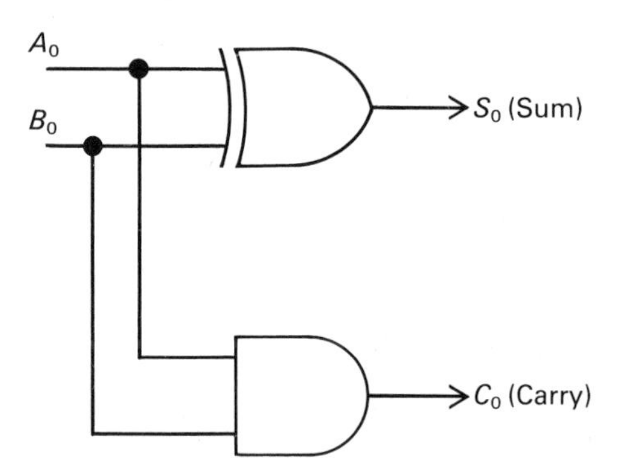

Fig. 4.3. Alternative implementation of half-adder circuit.

The full adder

The concept of binary addition can now be extended to handle 2-bit binary numbers. This gives sixteen possible combinations to be considered, too many to include here, but three cases are covered to indicate the technique (cf. Fig. 4.4).

A_1A_0	01	01	11
$+B_1B_0$	+00	+01	+11
C_1C_0	0 0	0 1	1 1
S_1S_0	01	10	10

Fig. 4.4. 2-bit binary addition.

The first operation to add A_0 and B_0 together has been discussed previously. The carry bit, C_0 which is produced is then passed on to the next stage. The second operation is for A_1 to be added to B_1, and to C_0. This means that three single-bit numbers have to be added together in the second stage to produce the sum S_1 and the carry bit C_1. A diagram showing how the two operations interact is shown in Fig. 4.5.

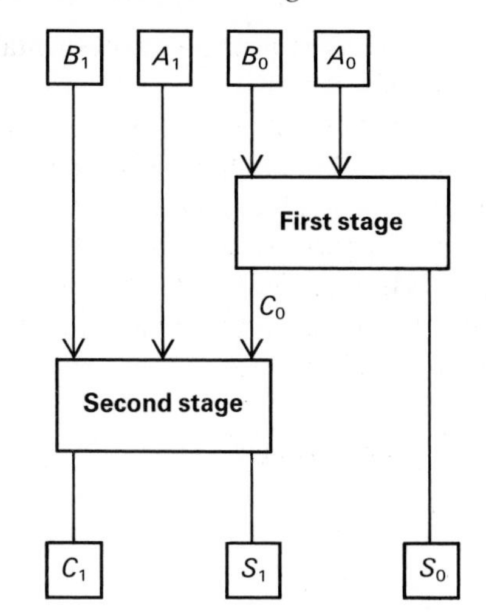

Fig. 4.5. Two-stage addition.

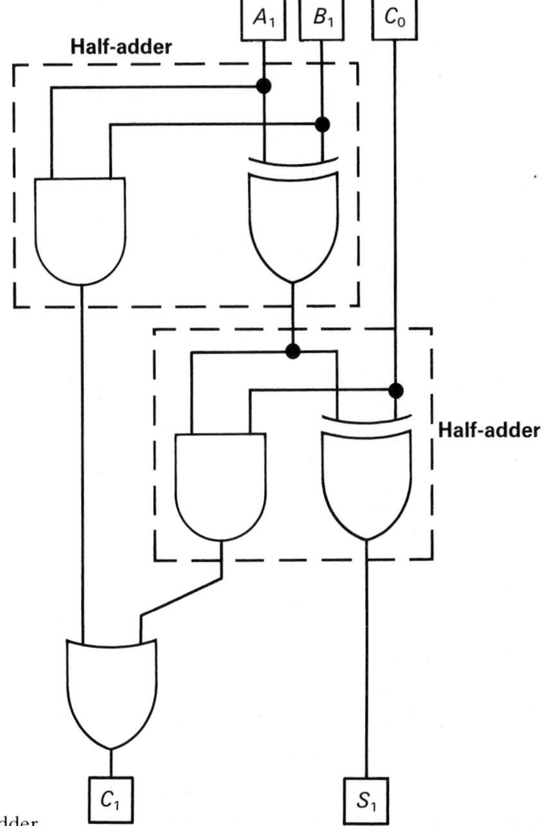

Fig. 4.6. Full adder.

It has already been shown that the first stage, known as the half-adder circuit, can be implemented using a combination of logic gates. The circuit for the second stage can be derived in exactly the same way by forming the truth table for each possible combination of the three inputs A_1, B_1 and C_0, and then deriving the Boolean equations from the table.

This circuit is known as a *full adder* and one common implementation is shown in Fig. 4.6. It should be noticed that it is in fact a combination of two half-adder circuits and it is this feature which gives rise to its name.

It is now possible to produce a complete logic unit which is capable of adding two double-bit binary numbers together and this is shown in Fig. 4.7.

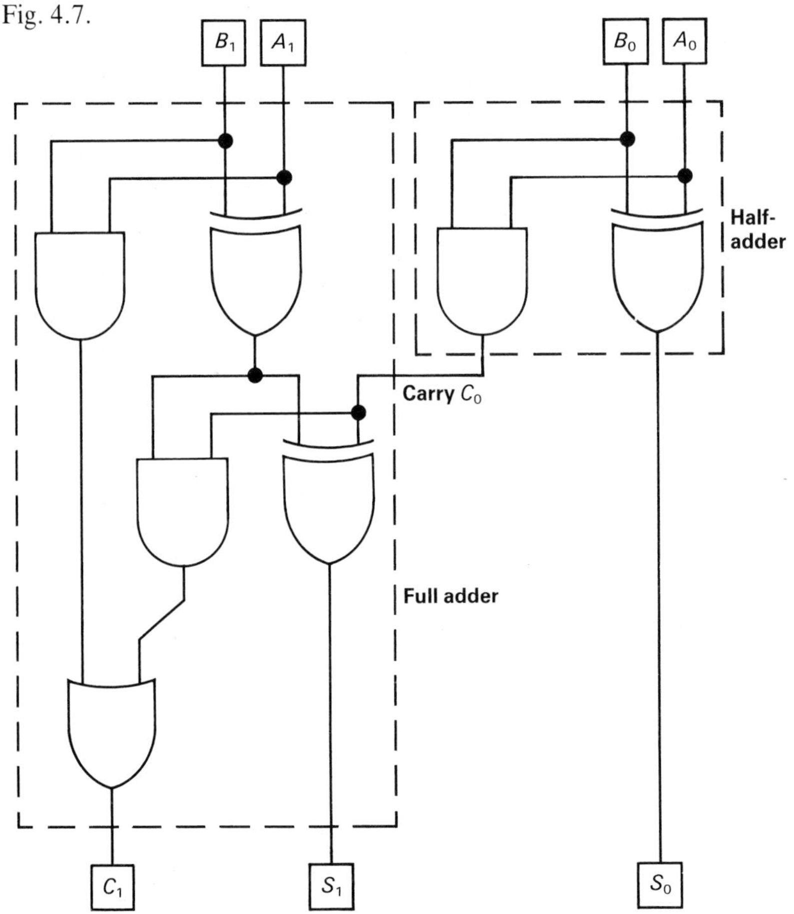

Fig. 4.7. A two-stage binary adder.

N-stage addition unit

If the binary numbers A and B contained more than 2 bits each, the techniques described above could easily be applied. Every additional stage would still only have to add 3 bits together, A_N, B_N and C_{N-1}, where N represents the current stage and $N-1$ represents the previous stage in the addition.

An example of a four-stage binary adder circuit is shown in Fig. 4.8.

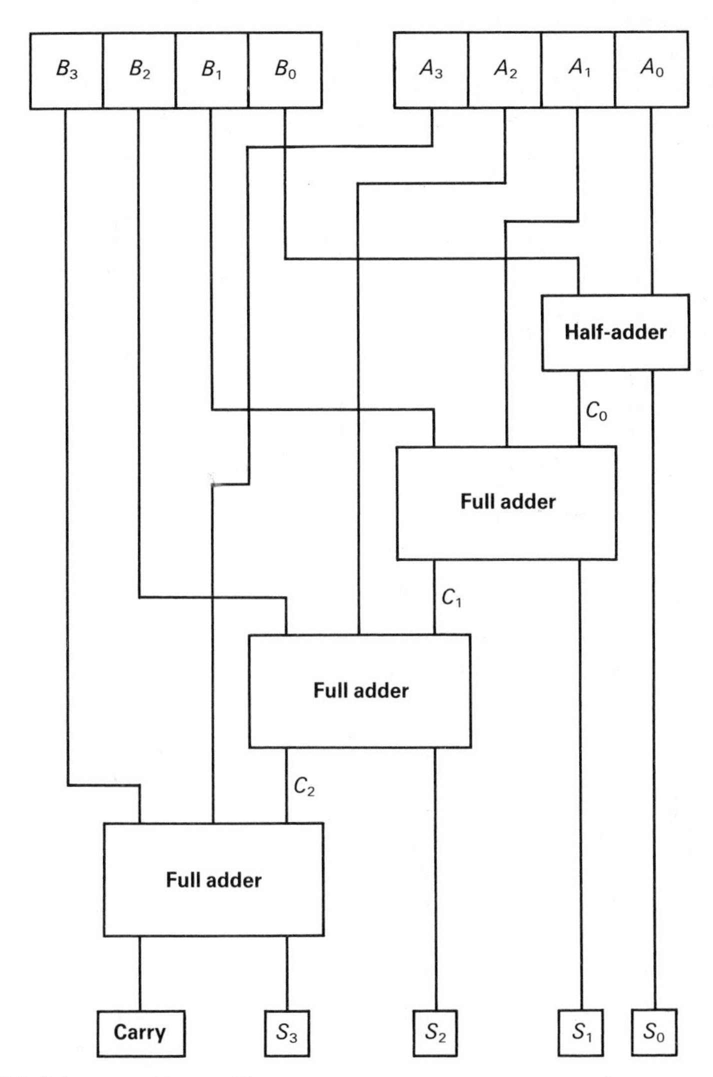

Fig. 4.8. A four-stage binary adder.

4.3 BINARY SUBTRACTION

Binary subtraction is performed by the operation $A+(-B)$. This is achieved by:

(i) taking the two's complement of the number B; and
(ii) adding the result to the number A.

The two's complement of a number can be produced by inverting the number and then incrementing the result by 1.

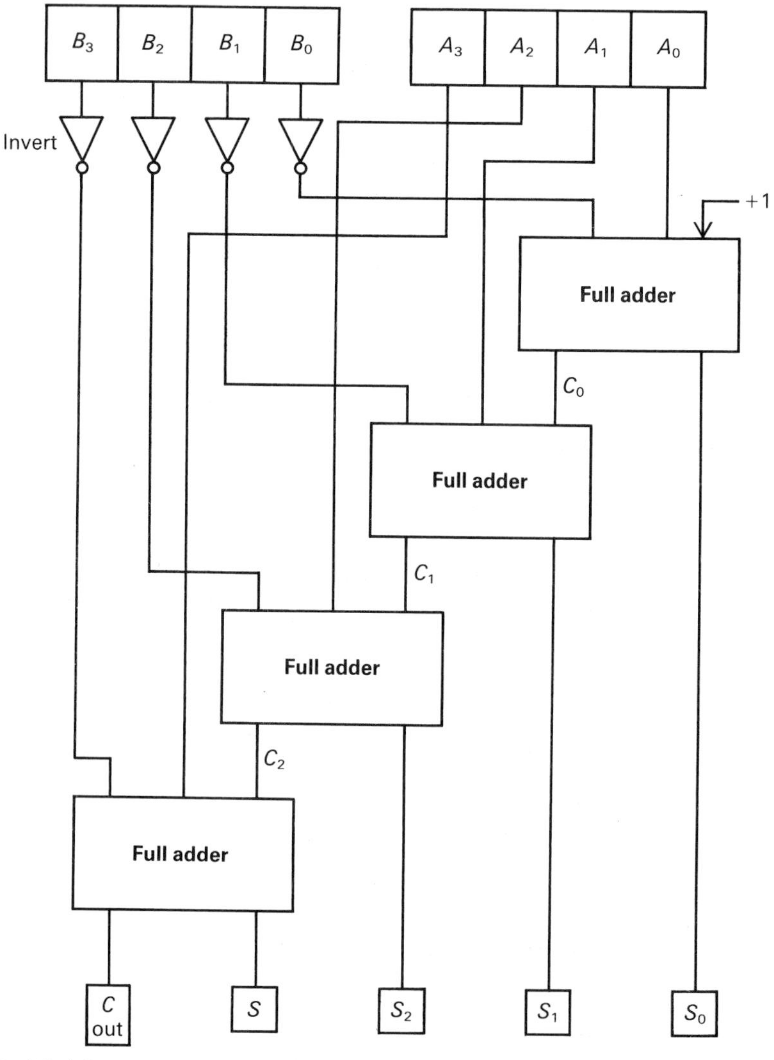

Fig. 4.9. A four-stage binary substraction unit.

The sequence in which this procedure is carried out can however, be altered without affecting the final result, and this is used in the hardware implementation of subtraction. The sequence of events in a hardware subtraction unit is:

(i) The number A is incremented by 1 by using a full adder instead of a half-adder in the least significant stage.

(ii) Each bit of the number B is inverted.

(iii) The results of stage (i) and (ii) are then added together.

A 4-bit binary subtraction unit is shown in Fig. 4.9.

4.4 SIMPLE ARITHMETIC UNIT

By comparing the four-stage adder circuit in Fig. 4.8 with the four-stage subtraction unit in Fig. 4.9, it will be noticed that a large portion of the

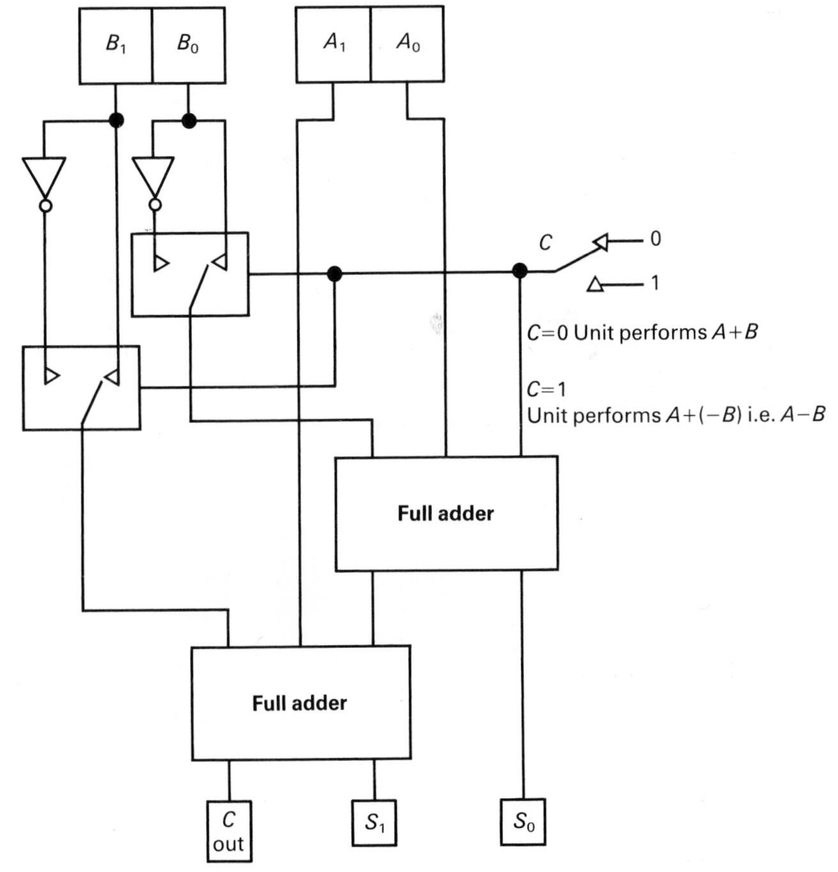

Fig. 4.10. A two-stage binary addition/subtraction unit.

hardware used is common. It is, therefore normal practice to combine these two circuits with some additional control logic to produce the simple arithmetic unit shown in Fig. 4.10.

When the control signal C is 0 the switches are in the position shown in the diagram, the number B is connected directly to the full adders, and a 0 is fed into the least significant full adder. The unit will, therefore, *add* A and B together. If however, the control signal C is 1 then the switches will change over and connect the inverse of B to the full adder and a 1 will be fed into the least significant full adder. The number B will thus be *subtracted* from A. The change-over switches used on the output of the number B are shown for explanatory purposes only, in a realistic circuit they could be replaced by multiplexers which are discussed in Chapter 5.

In all of the circuits described in this chapter sufficient time must be allowed for the logic gates to operate before the result is read. This is due to the propogation delay which is present in each gate.

4.5 COMPARATORS

As well as the normal arithmetic operations that have already been discussed, an ALU will usually include COMPARATOR circuits. These compare one binary number with another and indicate if they are equal, or if one is bigger than the other. In fact there are five possible comparisons of A and B that are normally included, these are:

(i)	Is A equal to B	$A = B$
(ii)	Is A greater than B	$A > B$
(iii)	Is A less than B	$A < B$
(iv)	Is A greater than or equal to B	$A \geqslant B$
(v)	Is A less than or equal to B	$A \leqslant B$

The design of logic circuits to implement these comparator functions is now considered.

Equal to comparator

A simple case is when A and B are 1-bit numbers and an output Z_E is required to indicate when A is equal to B.

A truth table can be drawn in the normal way to summarize the relationship between the inputs and outputs of the circuit, this is shown in Table 4.2.

Table 4.2. Truth table for 1-bit comparator.

A	B	Z_E
0	0	1
0	1	0
1	0	0
1	1	1

The Boolean equation can now be written as

$$Z_E = \bar{A}.\bar{B} + A.B$$

This can be implemented directly using AND and OR gates, as shown in Fig. 4.11, or it can be manipulated using De Morgan's Law to obtain a NAND gate solution.

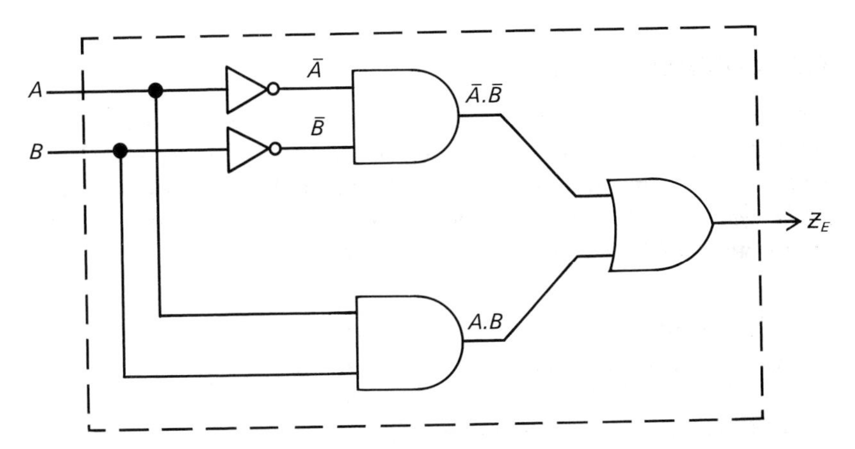

Fig. 4.11. Logic circuit for a 1-bit comparator.

This design can readily be extended to accomodate word lengths of any number of bits for A and B. The basic building block is still the 1-bit circuit shown in Fig. 4.11, with one of these circuits being allocated to each pair of corresponding bits in A and B. However, the final circuit must provide only one output Z_E to indicate when all of the corresponding pairs of bits are equal. This means that all of the outputs from the individual comparator stages must be 1 and these must be combined in one final AND gate at the output, as shown in Fig. 4.12.

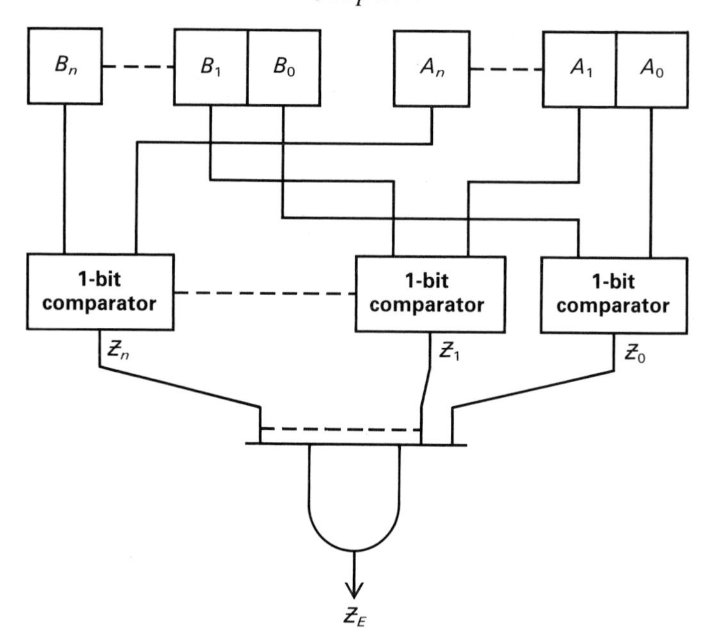

Fig. 4.12. *N*-bit comparator unit.

Greater than or equal to comparator

A more difficult design case to consider is when an output Z_{GE} is required to indicate that the number A is greater than or equal to B. It is now not possible to consider each pair of bits in isolation as in Section 4.1 and the design must be carried out for the specified number of bits in the numbers A and B.

In this example it is assumed that A and B are 2-bit numbers and a truth table for the circuit is shown in Table 4.3.

Because this is a more complex design problem it is essential to consider using the minimization techniques described in Chapter 2. A Karnaugh map for the problem is shown in Fig. 4.13.

It is apparent from this that there are many more 1's in the map than 0's and it is a good example of a situation where the inverse design technique could be applied.

This means that from now on the 0's in the diagram are considered rather than the 1's and a solution is shown in Fig. 4.14. From this the minimized Boolean equation for Z_{GE} can be written as

$$\bar{Z}_{GE} = \bar{A}_1.B_1 + \bar{A}_1.\bar{A}_0.B_0 + \bar{A}_0.B_1.B_0$$

Once again this can be implemented directly using AND and OR gates with an additional final inversion to produce the desired output Z_{GE}.

Table 4.3. Truth table for 2-bit comparator.

A_1	A_0	B_1	B_0	Z_{GE}
0	0	0	0	1
0	0	0	1	0
0	0	1	0	0
0	0	1	1	0
0	1	0	0	1
0	1	0	1	1
0	1	1	0	0
0	1	1	1	0
1	0	0	0	1
1	0	0	1	1
1	0	1	0	1
1	0	1	1	0
1	1	0	0	1
1	1	0	1	1
1	1	1	0	1
1	1	1	1	1

B_1B_0 \ A_1A_0	00	01	11	10
00	1	1	1	1
01	0	1	1	1
11	0	0	1	0
10	0	0	1	1

Fig. 4.13. Karnaugh map for 2-bit comparator.

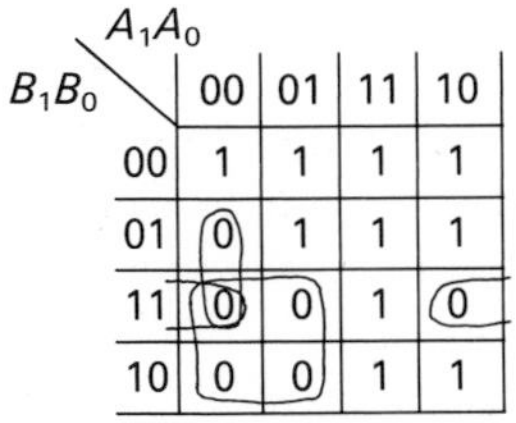

B_1B_0 \ A_1A_0	00	01	11	10
00	1	1	1	1
01	0	1	1	1
11	0	0	1	0
10	0	0	1	1

Fig. 4.14. Inverse design using a Karnaugh map.

Alternatively, it can be manipulated using De Morgan's Law to produce the NAND gate solution, as shown below,

$$Z_{GE} = \bar{\bar{Z}}_{GE} = \overline{\bar{A}_1.B_1 + \bar{A}_1.\bar{A}_0.B_0 + \bar{A}_0.B_1.B_0}$$
$$= \overline{\bar{A}_1.B_1} \,.\, \overline{\bar{A}_1.\bar{A}_0.B_0} \,.\, \overline{\bar{A}_0.B_1.B_0}$$

This results in the logic circuit shown in Fig. 4.15.

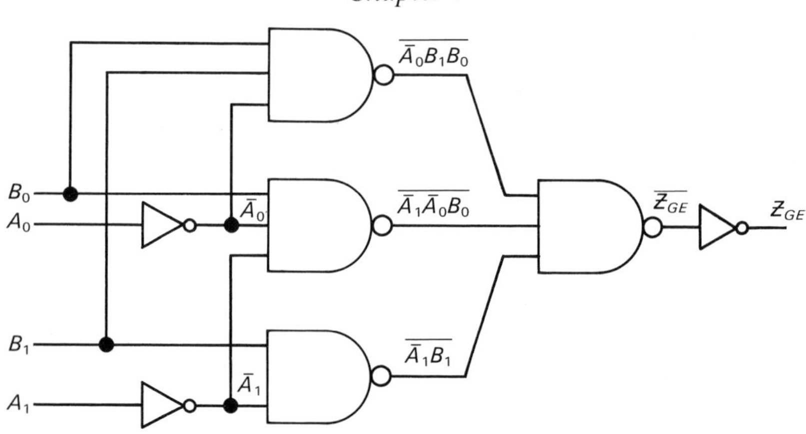

Fig. 4.15. Logic circuit for a 2-bit comparator.

Comparator units in a computer

Similar designs can be carried out for all of the possible comparator functions discussed earlier. In a computer these circuits would normally be integrated into one large comparator unit, with a separate output for each of the functions, as shown in Fig. 4.16. It is obviously possible to further minimize the number of logic gates required by sharing common parts of the circuits and by making use of relationships such as $Z_{GT} = \bar{Z}_{LE}$.

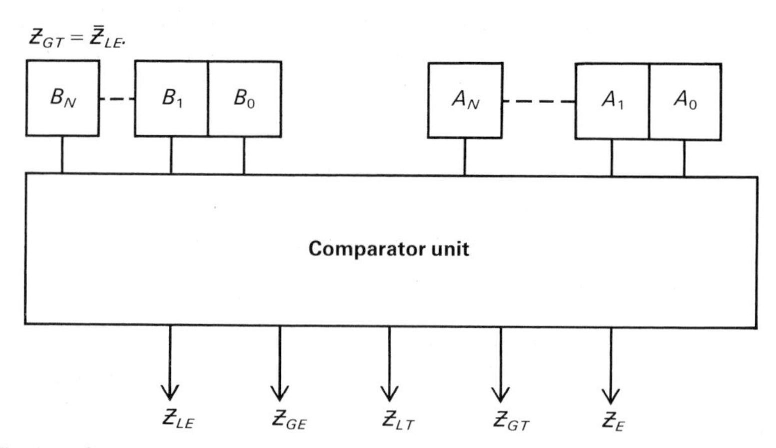

Fig. 4.16. Complete comparator unit.

4.6 SHIFTING

Another group of functions that is included within the ALU is concerned with the *shifting* of binary numbers to the left or to the right of their original position. A simple example is shown in Fig. 4.17, where a 4-bit number is shifted by one bit position to the right.

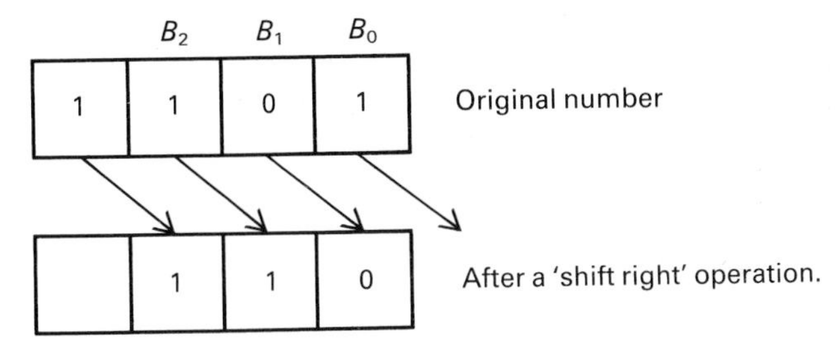

Fig. 4.17. Right shift operation.

Two questions must be answered before this operation is fully defined. Firstly, what happens to the least significant 1 when it has been shifted *out* of the original 4-bit word. Then secondly what, if anything, is fed into the most significant bit which is now empty. A number of alternative answers are possible to these questions, and these are now discussed in detail.

Rotate operation

If the least significant bit is fed back into the most significant bit of the word, then the operation is fully defined and is known as *rotate right* (cf. Fig. 4.18).

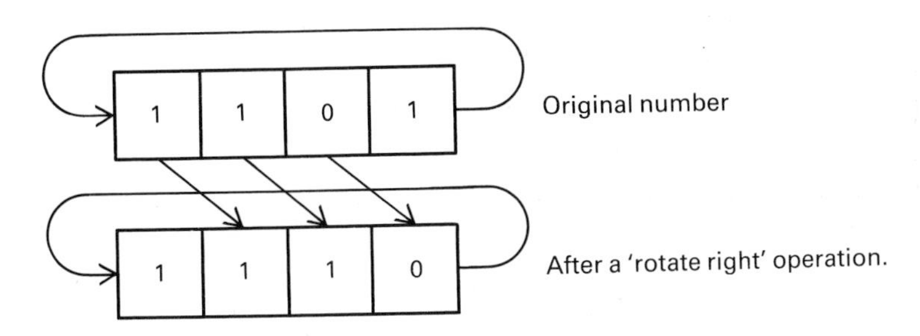

Fig. 4.18. Rotate right.

Logical shift operation

If the least significant bit is discarded completely or if it is held in a separate 1-bit store and if a 0 is fed into the most significant bit of the word, then the operation is known as a *logical shift right*. The optional 1-bit store is normally called the *carry bit* (*C*), (cf. Fig. 4.19).

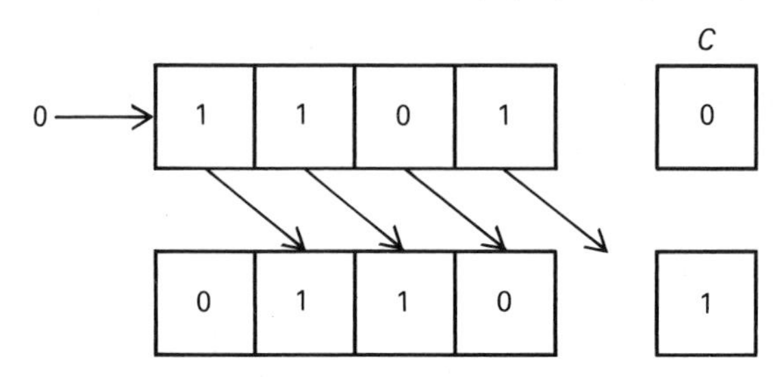

Fig. 4.19. Logical shift right.

Arithmetic shift operation

If the least significant bit is treated in the same way as in the logical shift but the most significant bit is fed back to itself then it is known as an *arithmetic shift right*. Connecting the most significant bit in this way ensures that the *sign* of the number will not change when the shift operation takes place. In other words a positive number will have an 0 fed in and remain positive while a negative number will have a 1 fed in and remain negative (cf. Fig. 4.20).

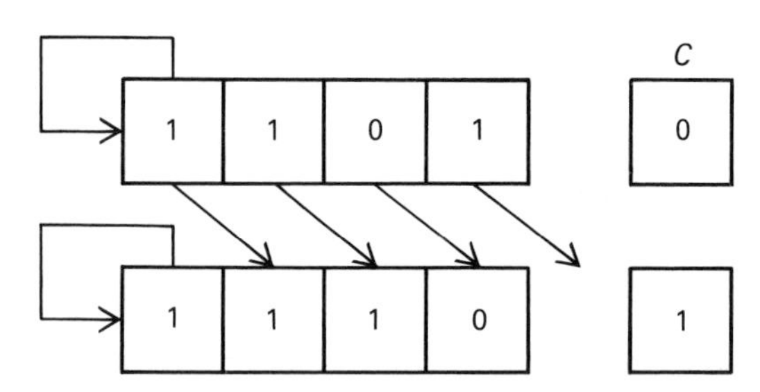

Fig. 4.20. Arithmetic shift right.

Shift left operations

The rotate and logical shift operations can be carried out for functions which require a shift to the left instead of to the right and these are shown in Fig. 4.21. A left arithmetic shift operation is equivalent to a logical left shift and is not normally used.

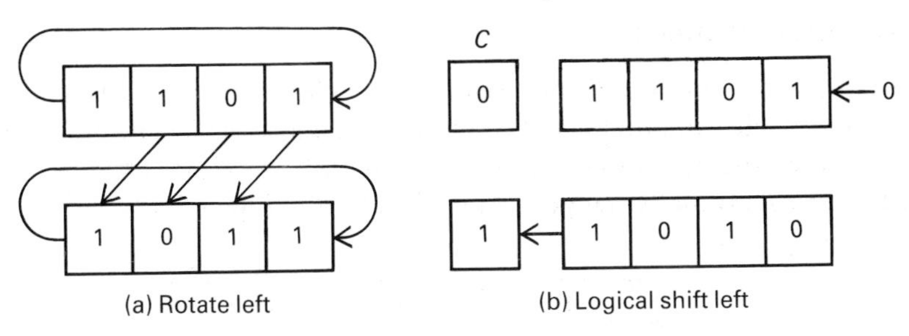

Fig. 4.21. Rotate and logic shift left.

Rotate through carry

All of these shift operations are normally implemented on even the smallest computer and can also be combined to produce more complex functions, such as *rotate right* through *carry* (cf. Fig. 4.22).

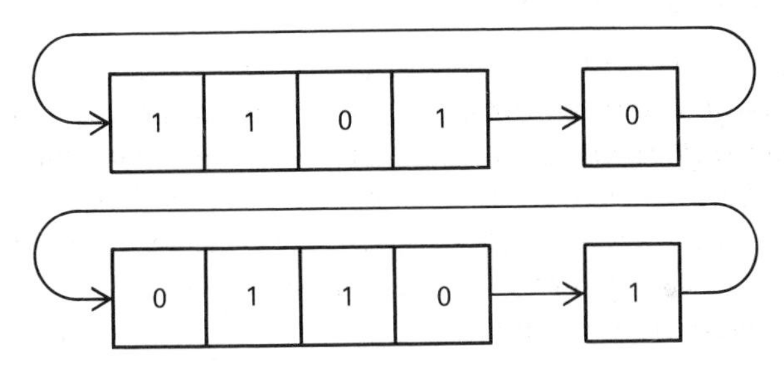

Fig. 4.22. Rotate right through carry.

In practice shift operations are often used in their own right but they can also form the basis of other arithmetic operations, such as multiply and divide.

4.7 MULTIPLICATION AND DIVISION

In large computers the multiply and divide functions are implemented using additional hardware, but in smaller computers often only the basic functions of *add, subtract, compare* and *shift* are implemented. In order to perform multiplication a program has to be written which uses repeated addition operations instead, e.g. 4×3 is replaced with $4 + 4 + 4$. Division is treated in a similar way and can be replaced with repeated subtraction operations.

4.8 COMPLETE ARITHMETIC AND LOGIC UNIT

If all of the functions described in this chapter were brought together they would form a complete ALU. Most of the operations that it would carry out would require two binary numbers to be present at the input to the unit and then one of the control inputs would be used to select the operation to be performed (cf. Fig. 4.23).

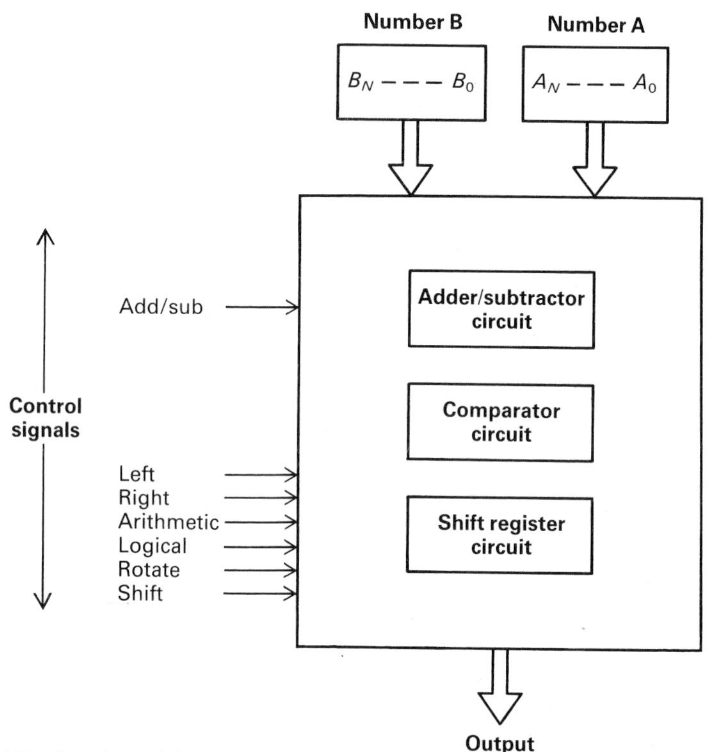

Fig. 4.23. Complete arithmetic and logic unit.

When the operation is completed the result will be available at the output of the unit.

It is important to realize that there is a time delay between the operation being started and the correct result appearing at the output. This is due to each gate within the unit having a certain propogation delay, usually measured in nanoseconds (10^{-9} seconds). Any further processing which is to be carried out on this result must wait for the correct period of time before proceeding. The accurate timing of the control pulses is vital for correct operation of the unit. This is taken care of within the control unit which is described in Chapter 7.

Chapter 5

Decoders and Multiplexers

5.1 INTRODUCTION

This chapter describes the use of combinational logic in circuits which are designed to encode and decode binary information and to control the transmission of binary information between two points using multiplexing/demultiplexing techniques.

In each case a suitable logic circuit is designed and then a typical application within a computer is described.

5.2 DECODER CIRCUITS

The input to a decoder is data coded in a way which specifies which of a number of output lines is to be set to logical 1.

The binary decoder

One of the simplest forms of decoder is the binary decoder. In a 3-bit binary decoder the 3-bit binary number representing the decimal

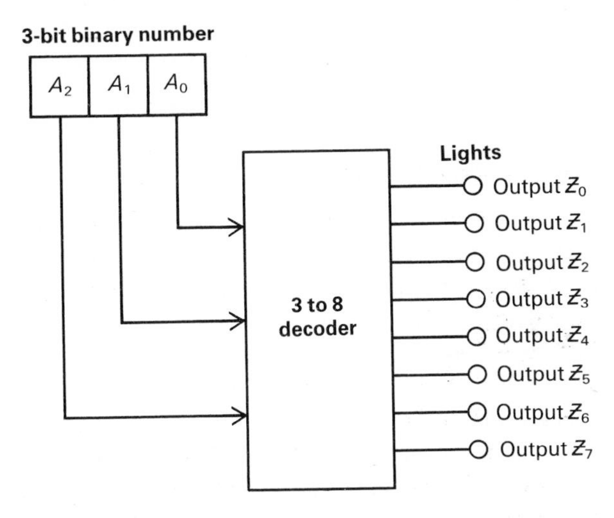

Fig. 5.1. Decoder example.

numbers 0 to 7 is input to the decoder circuitry. This is designed to decode it to produce an output on one of eight seperate output lines representing the numbers 0 to 7 as shown in Fig. 5.1. This circuit is called a 3-to-8 decoder.

Table 5.1. 3-to-8 decoder outputs

A_2	A_1	A_0	Z_7	Z_6	Z_5	Z_4	Z_3	Z_2	Z_1	Z_0
0	0	0	0	0	0	0	0	0	0	1
0	0	1	0	0	0	0	0	0	1	0
0	1	0	0	0	0	0	0	1	0	0
0	1	1	0	0	0	0	1	0	0	0
1	0	0	0	0	0	1	0	0	0	0
1	0	1	0	0	1	0	0	0	0	0
1	1	0	0	1	0	0	0	0	0	0
1	1	1	1	0	0	0	0	0	0	0

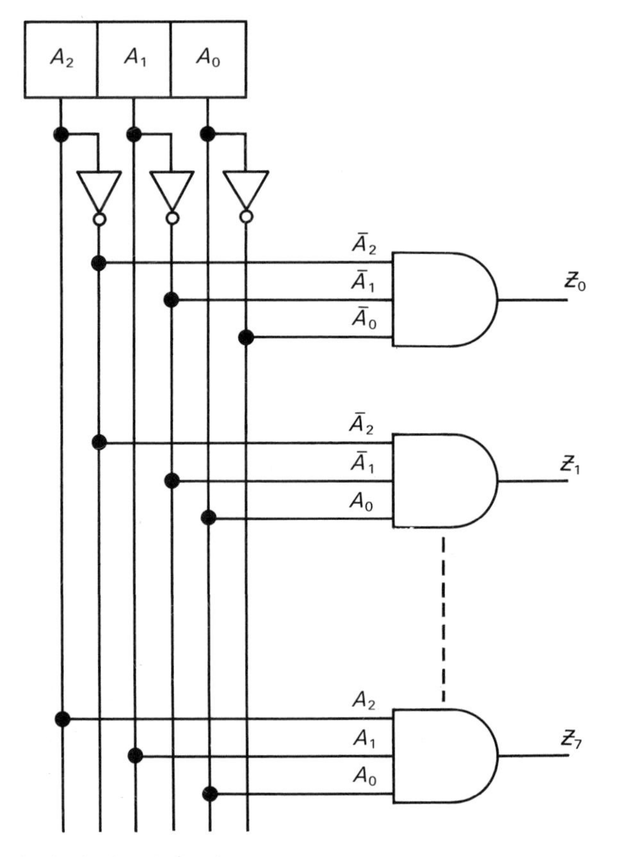

Fig. 5.2. Logic circuits for 3-to-8 decoder.

Only one of the outputs would be on at any one time, indicating the current value of the 3-bit binary number. For example if the binary number at the input was 010, then output Z_2 would be a 1. A summary of the operation of tpplicatihe lamps is shown in Table 5.1.

In designing a logic circuit to meet this specification it is best to take one output at a time. Starting with the output Z_0, this line would be in logic 1 state *only* when the binary number was 000, i.e. all three input lines are at logical 0. In Boolean algebra this would be written as $Z_0 = \bar{A}_2.\bar{A}_1.\bar{A}_0$. The next output Z_1 be in logic 1 state only when the input number was 001, giving the Boolean equation $Z_0 = \bar{A}_2.\bar{A}_1.A_0$. The remaining outputs would be processed in the same way, giving a total of eight simple Boolean equations which can readily be implemented in logic gates as shown in Fig. 5.2.

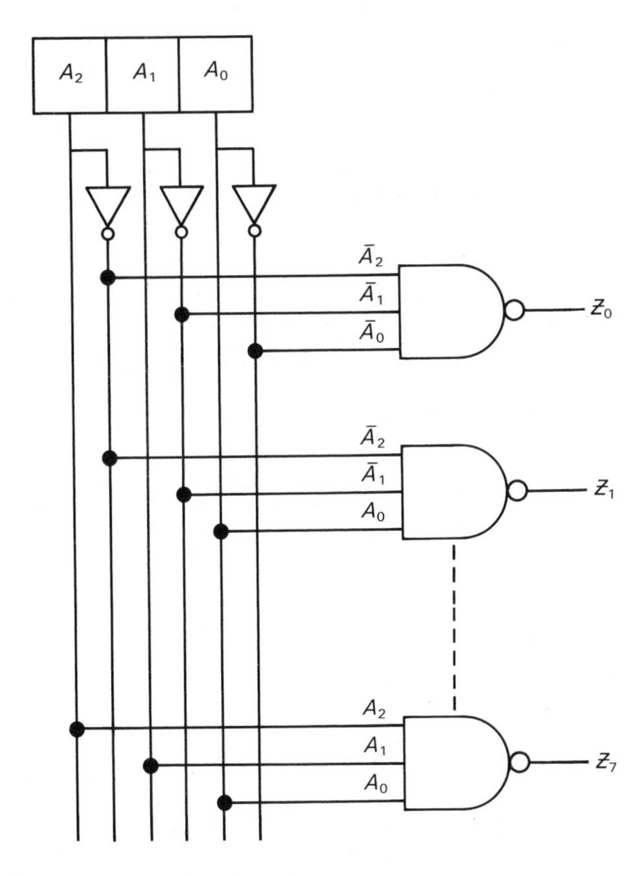

Fig. 5.3. NAND gate circuit for 3-to-8 decoder.

In many instances manufacturers have used NAND gates instead of AND gates in the final stage, see Fig. 5.3. This results in the decoded output being in the logic 0 state when it is active and the remaining outputs being at logic 1.

In theory, decoders may be of any size but there is a practical limit to the number of inputs to a single NAND gate that can be achieved. In standard small scale integrated circuits (SSI) there is a maximum of eight inputs to a gate. One very common range of SSI chips is the 74 series which includes an eight input NAND gate known as the 7430.

It is also possible to obtain complete decoding circuits on a single chip. For example the circuit shown in Fig. 5.3 forms the basis of the 3:8 decoder, type 74138. One obvious restriction on the size of decoder that can be implemented in this way is the number of pins that have to be accommodated around the edge of the chip. For many years the standard number of pins on an SSI chip was either fourteen or sixteen. However, with the advent of MSI and the LSI technology this number has greatly increased and now ranges up to devices with sixty-four pins.

Decoder applications

There are many areas within a digital computer in which decoder circuits are used. One good example which clearly illustrates their use is

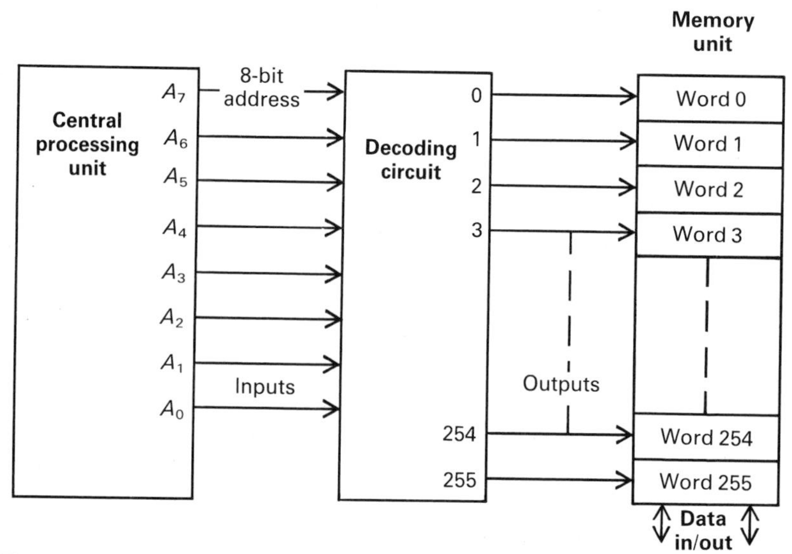

Fig. 5.4. Memory addressing.

in the area of memory addressing. The central processing unit of the computer sends a binary number, called an address, to the memory unit. Each word held in the memory has a unique address associated with it. The address must, therefore, pick out only one of the many words stored in the memory and it is a decoder circuit which enables it to do this. For example if a small computer had a memory of 256 words, this would require an 8-bit binary number for the address. A block diagram of this system is shown in Fig. 5.4. The decoding circuit required is a straight forward extension of that shown in Fig. 5.3 having eight inputs and 256 outputs. A portion of this circuit is shown in Fig. 5.5.

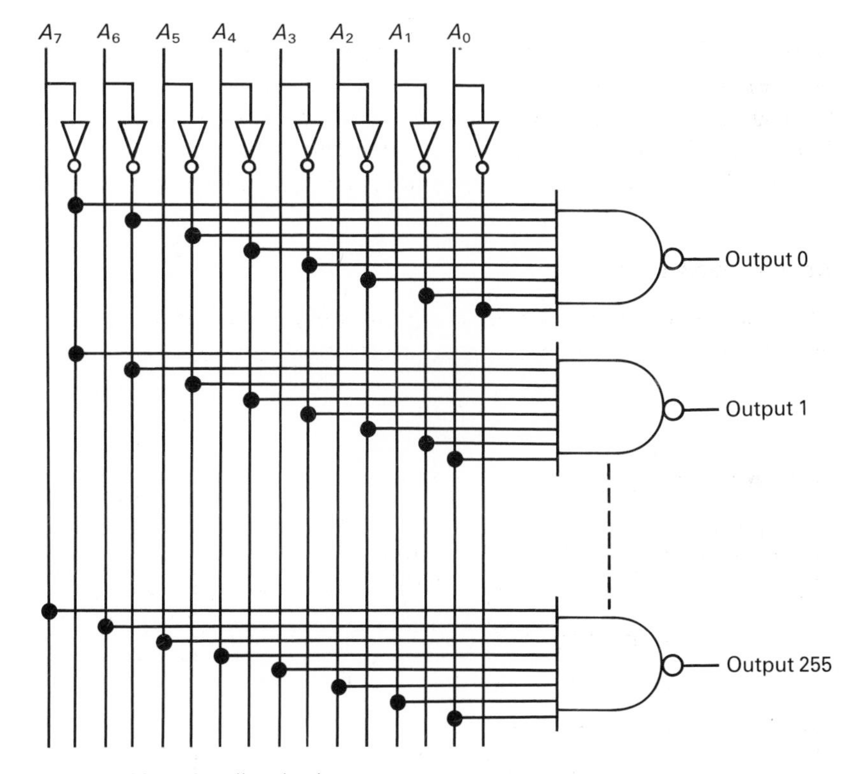

Fig. 5.5. Address decoding circuit.

A few years ago this circuit would have been implemented using SSI devices with a considerable amount of work being involved in connecting all of the pins. However, in most memory units that are manufactured today the decoding circuitry is included on the same LSI chip as the memory words themselves. The interconnections are, therefore, all taken care of in the internal layout of the chip and the only external connections required are those for the address and data information and a few control signals.

5.3 ENCODER CIRCUITS

An encoder circuit performs the opposite function to that of a decoder in that it has many individual input lines and the output is a coded pattern identifying each of the inputs.

Binary encoder

The simplest form of encoder is the 2-bit binary encoder with enable shown in Fig. 5.6 below.

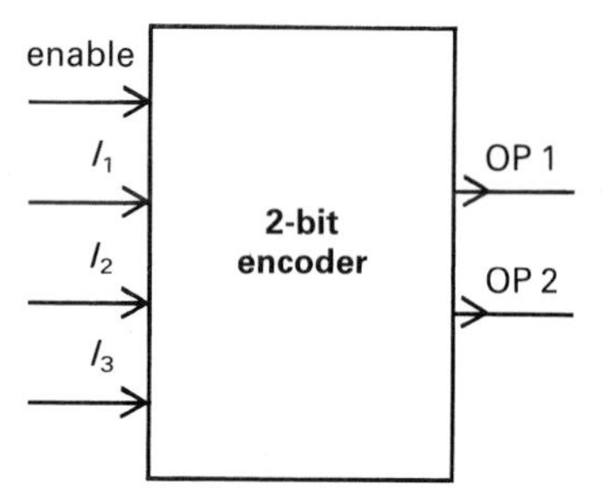

Fig. 5.6. A 2-bit binary decoder.

Only one of the three input lines can be a 1 at any time and the output (when the circuit is enabled) is the binary pattern representing the input line number (cf. Table 5.2).

Table 5.2. Truth table for a 2-bit binary encoder.

I_3	I_2	I_1	enable	$OP2$	$OP1$
X	X	X	0	0	0
0	0	1	1	0	1
0	1	0	1	1	0
1	0	0	1	1	1

X = don't care

Priority encoders

In the circuit described above it is assumed that only one input line will be a logical 1 at any time. If more than one line is a 1 the circuit must decide which input is of the highest priority and set the output accordingly. The function for a 2-bit binary priority encoder is given in Table 5.3.

Table 5.3. Truth table for a 2-bit priority encoder.

I_3	I_2	I_1	enable	$OP2$	$OP1$
X	X	X	0	0	0
0	0	1	1	0	1
0	1	0	1	1	0
0	1	1	1	1	0
1	0	0	1	1	1
1	0	1	1	1	1
1	1	0	1	1	1
1	1	1	1	1	1

X = don't care.

The output is the binary pattern representing the highest numbered input line which is 1.

The Karnaugh maps for the two outputs are shown in Fig. 5.7.

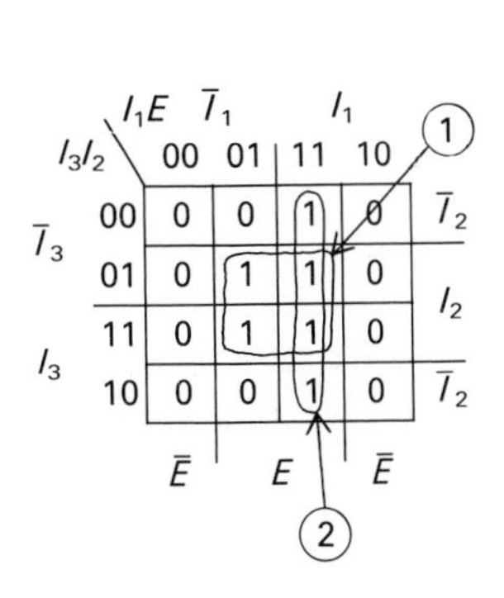

Karnaugh Map for *OP2*

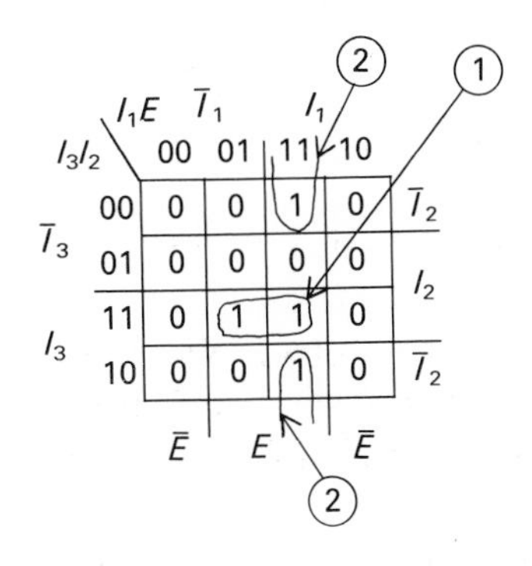

Karnaugh Map for *OP1*

Fig. 5.7. Karnaugh maps for a 2-bit priority encoder.

From the Karnaugh maps

$$OP1 = I_3I_2E + \bar{I}_2I_1E$$
$$OP2 = I_2E + I_1E$$

And by using the Law of Double Negation and De Morgan's Law the outputs are given by

$$OP1 = \overline{\overline{I_3 I_2 E} \,.\, \overline{\bar{I}_2 I_1 E}}$$

$$OP2 = \overline{\overline{I_2 E} \,.\, \overline{I_1 E}}$$

Which gives the circuit shown in Fig. 5.8.

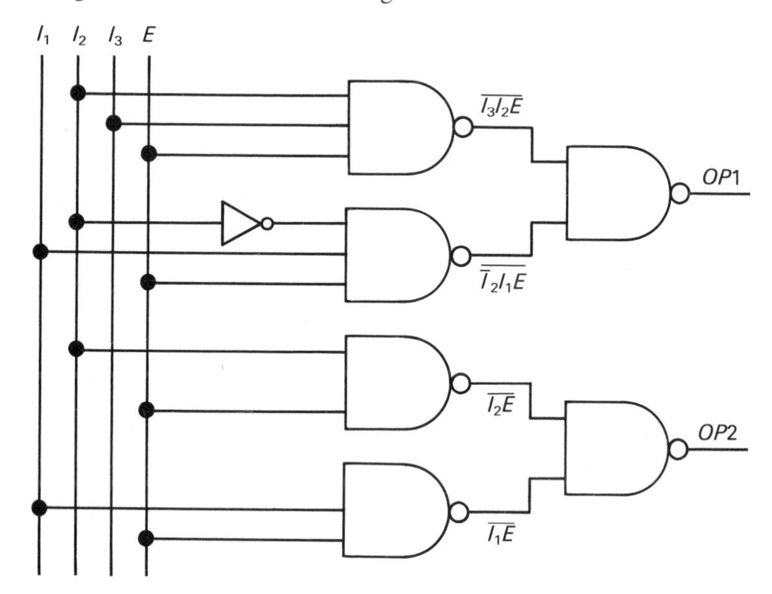

Fig. 5.8. Circuit diagram for a 2-bit priority encoder.

In a similar way 3-bit and 4-bit priority encoders, with seven inputs and fifteen inputs respectively can be designed.

Application of priority encoders

Priority encoders are used to connect a number of single bit inputs (switches) to the data bus of a computer system. They enable many switches to be connected to the data bus and for the computer to obtain the identification number of the highest priority switch which is closed by simply reading the data bus.

5.4 MULTIPLEXERS AND DEMULTIPLEXERS

When used together these circuits enable several sources of information to share a common transmission path on the way to separate destinations. For example, if there was a single telephone line between point

A and point *B* but there were four telephones at each end. Only one pair of telephones could be connected at one time as shown in Fig. 5.9. When that conversation had been completed the multiplexer and demultiplexer would be free to move on and connect another pair of telephones together. This results in the telephone line being *time shared* between the telephones, and people wanting to make a telephone call having to wait their turn.

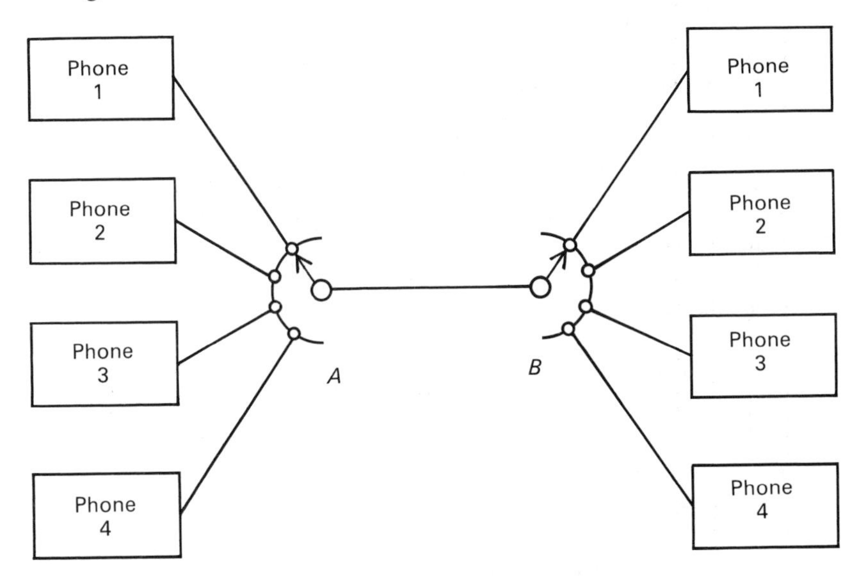

Fig. 5.9. Telephone multiplexer/demultiplexer example.

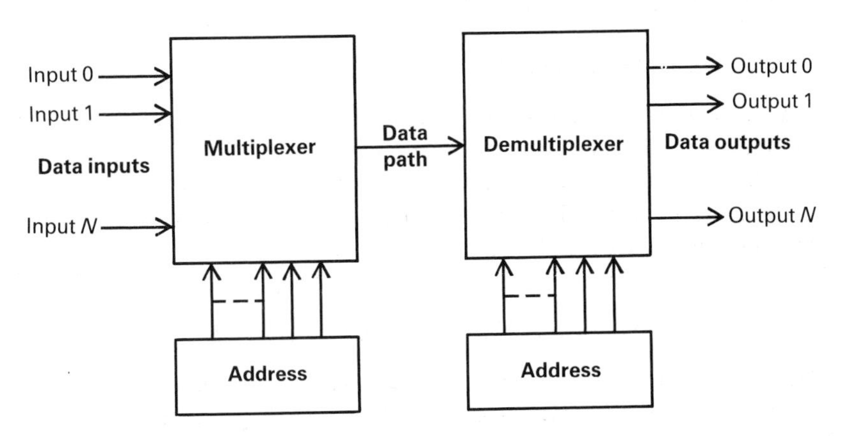

Fig. 5.10. Multiplexer/demultiplexer block diagram.

In most computer applications the multiplexer and demultiplexer are synchronized and change from one channel to another in unison. This means that input 0 will always be connected to output 0, input 1 will be connected to output 1 etc. and so on. The choice of which matched pair to connect together is made by the *address* that is fed to the multiplexer and demultiplexer units, as shown in Fig. 5.10.

Multiplexer circuit

The address can be thought of as simply a binary number which must be *decoded* to produce only one enable signal at a time. This decoder circuit would be identical to that described in Section 5.2, 'The Binary Decoder'. The enable signal from the decoder is fed to a simple AND gate enable circuit and is used to select one of the input data lines. The outputs from all of these enable circuits can be fed into one OR gate because only one can possibly be selected at any point in time. From the output of the OR gate the signal is fed to the time-shared transmission path.

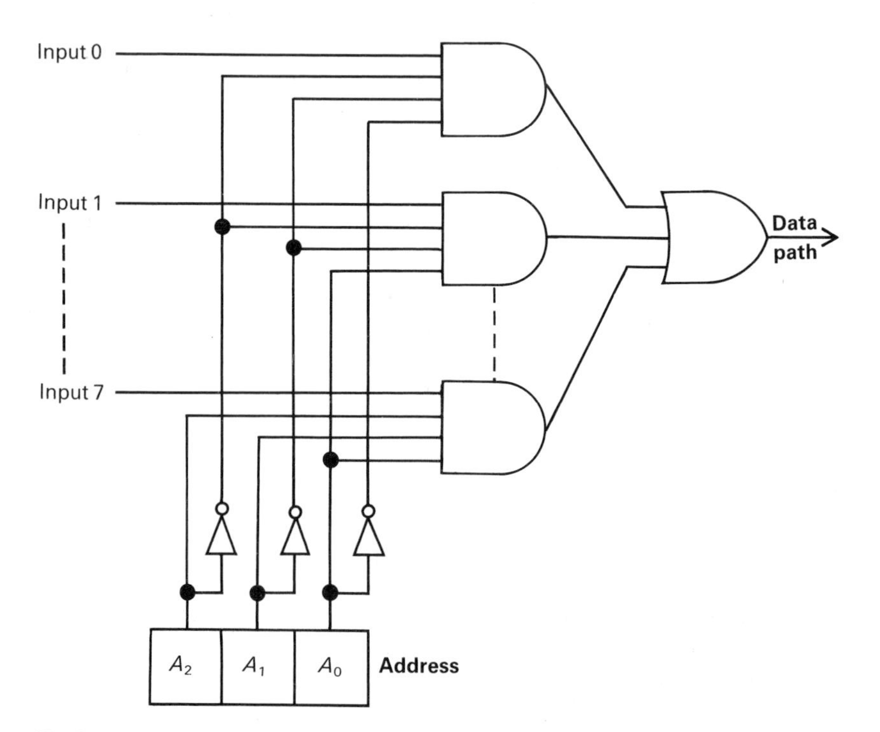

Fig. 5.11. Multiplexer circuit diagram.

The logic diagram can be simplified slightly by combining the enable AND gates with the decoding circuit as shown in Fig. 5.11, which has been designed for eight data inputs.

Demultiplexer circuit

A block diagram of a typical demultiplexer unit is shown in Fig. 5.12, the address decoding circuit is identical to that used in the multiplexer circuit and described in Section 5.2, 'The Binary Decoder'. In this case all the enable gates have one input fed from the shared transmission path. The data flowing along this path will thus pass through the selected enable gate to the correct data output line.

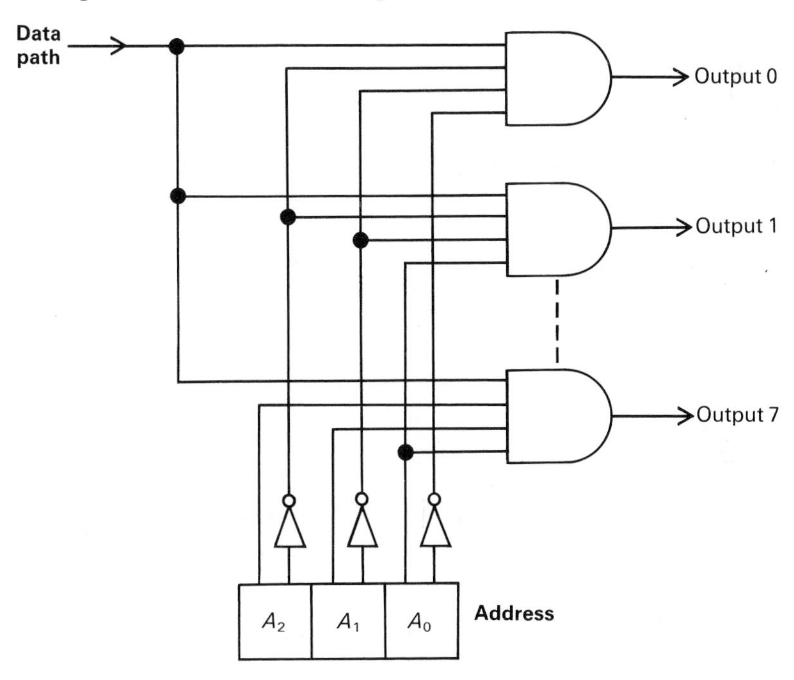

Fig. 5.12. Demultiplexer block diagram.

Applications of multiplexers and demultiplexers

Data transmission example. The complete data transmission system is shown in Fig. 5.13.

To ensure that the input data lines are correctly matched to the output data lines it is important that the two addresses are identical and change in step with each other. One simple way of achieving this is to

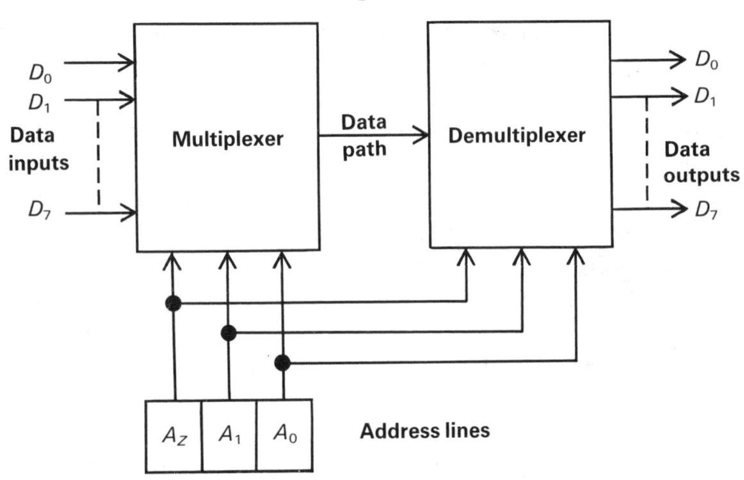

Fig. 5.13. Complete transmission system.

send the address from one end to the other by using additional lines between the multiplexer and demultiplexer. This is only really feasible over short distances and is shown in Fig. 5.13.

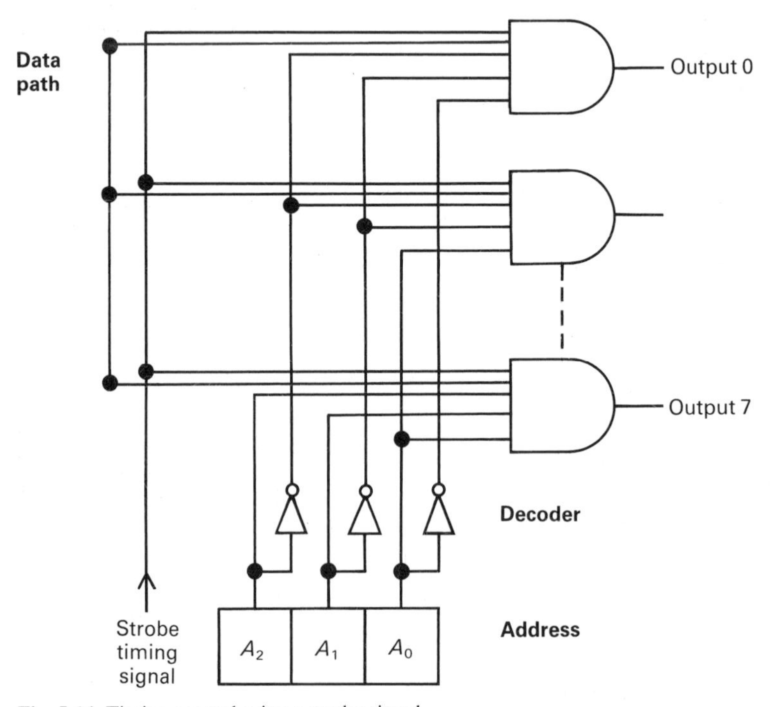

Fig. 5.14. Timing control using a strobe signal.

It is also important to stop any unwanted data being transmitted while the addresses are being changed. This can be achieved by using a *strobe* line which is an additional enable line connected to the decoder circuit. This signal is used to disable all of the decoder outputs until the new address has been set up when it can be enabled to allow the decoder to operate normally. A circuit which will achieve this is shown in Fig. 5.14. The timing of the strobe signal is important and highlights the importance of co-ordinating control signals in a digital system.

Computer bus example. Within a digital computer it is often necessary to connect the outputs of several logic gates onto one common line, known as a *bus* line. This is obviously a place where a multiplexer circuit would be of use.

The bus lines are normally grouped together, for example in a simple microcomputer the data is passed between the various units over an eight-line data bus. This means that eight multiplexers would be required in this application, one per bus line. A typical configuration is shown in Fig. 5.15.

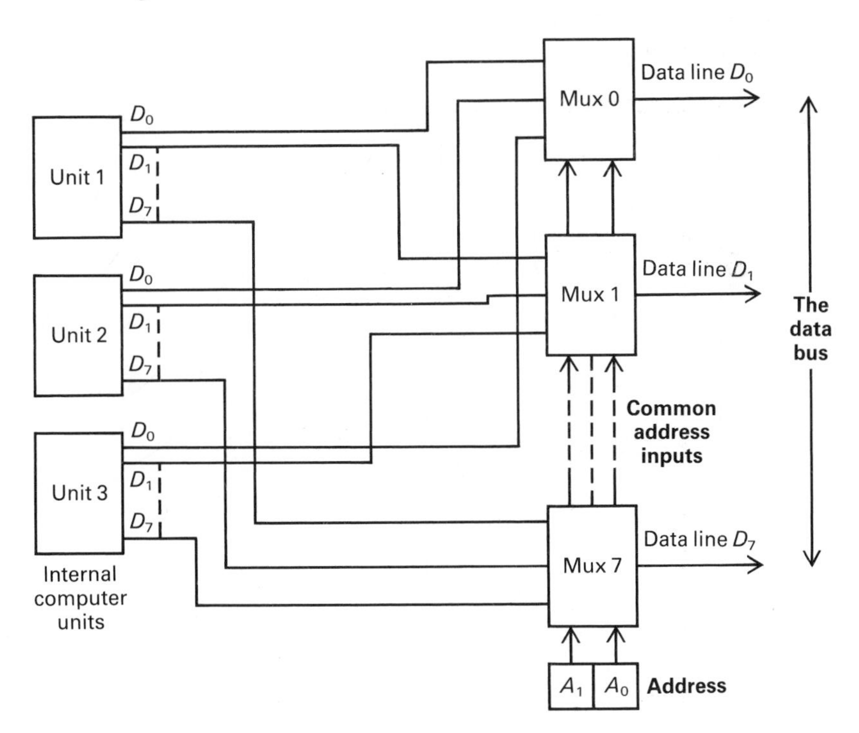

Fig. 5.15. Multiplexed computer data bus.

Chapter 6

Sequential Logic

6.1 INTRODUCTION

The output at any instant in time from a combinational logic circuit is a function of its current inputs. Many computer operations require circuits which have time-dependent properties, such as

(i) the output being a function of past as well as current inputs; and
(ii) the output being set to appear at a known time.

In this chapter the basic elements for sequential logic circuits will be described and their application in counters, registers and memories discussed.

6.2 THE J-K BISTABLE

The J-K Bistable (or J-K Flip Flop) is a logic element with properties which enable it to act as either a divide by two circuit or as a 1-bit store. The divide by two characteristics enable this element to form the building block for counters and shift registers, whilst the 1-bit store properties make it useful in registers and memories.

Figure 6.1 shows the diagrammatic representation of a J-K Flip Flop.

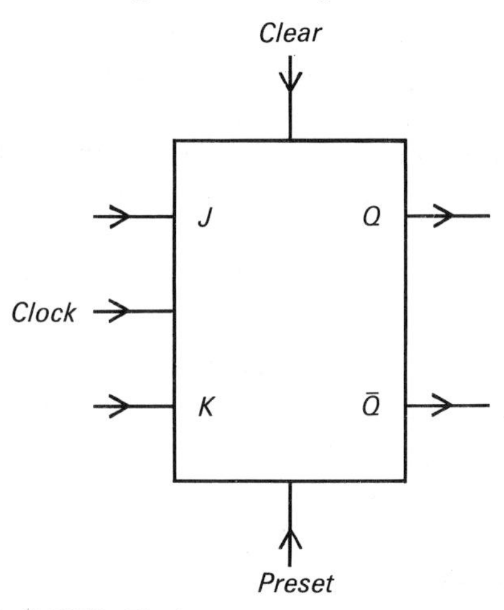

Fig. 6.1. A J-K Bistable (J-K Flip Flop).

There are five inputs, *J, K, Clock, Clear* and *Preset* and two outputs Q and its inverse $\bar{Q}$.

Divide by two characteristics

With logical 1's on the four inputs *J, K, Clear* and *Preset* the element acts as a divide by two circuit. The clock input consists of a series of pulses. The outputs Q and $\bar{Q}$ are also a series of pulses but at half the frequency of the input, the output changing state on the falling edge of the input, as shown in the timing diagram, Fig. 6.2.

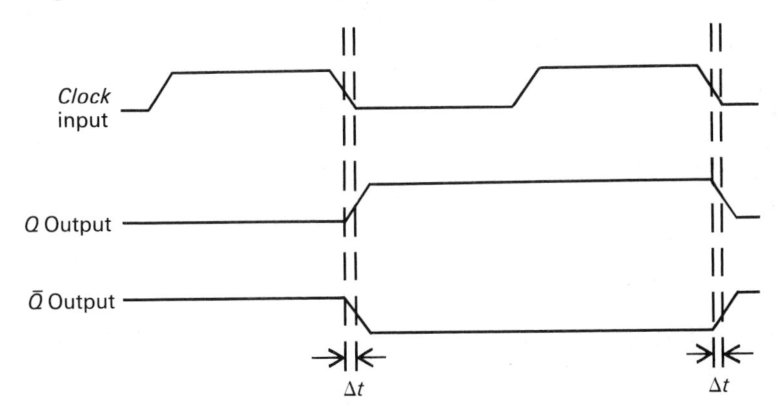

Fig. 6.2. 'Divide by two' characteristic.

The output occurs at a time Δt, the propagation delay, after the falling edge of the input.

The element is shown to be in the 0 state ($Q = 0$) prior to the first input clock pulse arriving. On the falling edge of this pulse corresponding changes occur in Q and $\bar{Q}$. Similarly the falling edge of the second clock pulse causes both outputs to revert to their original state. Thus one output pulse is produced for every two input clock pulses.

Initial conditions

The intial conditions of any circuit comprised of J-K Flip Flops sets initial conditions using the *Clear* and *Preset* inputs to the J-K.
Clear = 0 and *Preset* = 0 makes $Q = 1$ and $Q = 1$
Clear = 0 and *Preset* = 1 makes $Q = 0$ and $\bar{Q} = 1$
Clear = 1 and *Preset* = 0 makes $Q = 1$ and $\bar{Q} = 0$

The outputs are independant of *J, K* and *Clock* and change as soon as either *Clear* or *Preset* change.

1-bit store characteristics

The J and K inputs are used to enable the J-K Flip Flop to be used as a storage device.

With $J = 0$ and $K = 1$, Q is set to 0 and $\bar{Q}$ to 1 on the falling edge of the next clock pulse. Similarly with $J = 1$ and $K = 0$, Q is set to 1 and $\bar{Q}$ to 0 on the falling edge of the clock (cf. Fig. 6.3).

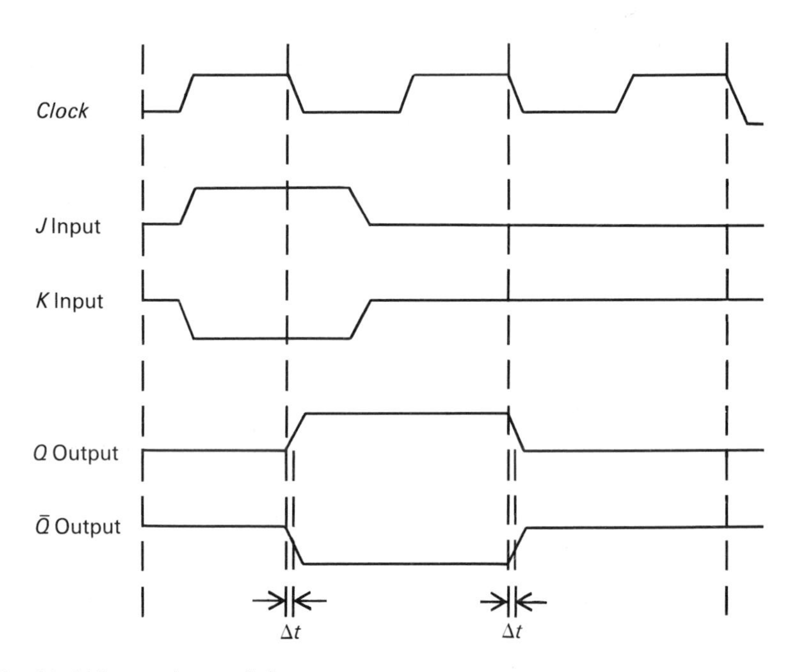

Fig. 6.3. 1-bit store characteristics.

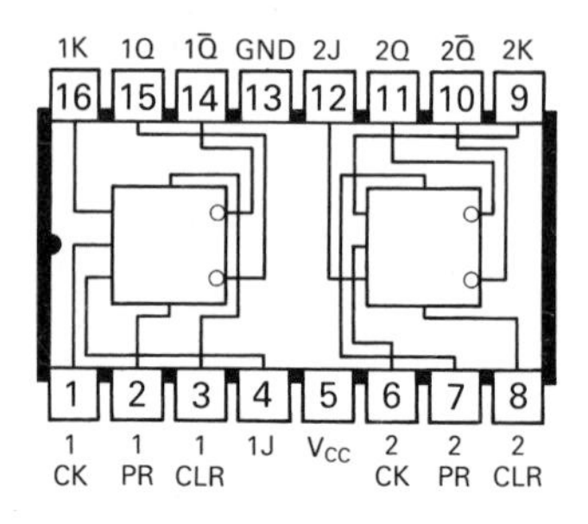

Fig. 6.4. SN7476 Dual J-K Flip Flop.

Integrated circuits

There are various integrated circuits containing J-K Bistables. The most common chip is an SN7476, Dual J-K Flip Flop as shown in Fig. 6.4.

6.3 COUNTERS

Counters are circuits which count pulses applied to the clock inputs of a series of bistables. A counter consisting of n bistables elements will count $2^n - 1$ pulses and then return to its original state after the next pulse. Counters can count in many different codes and can count either up or down by either adding or subtracting one for each input pulse.

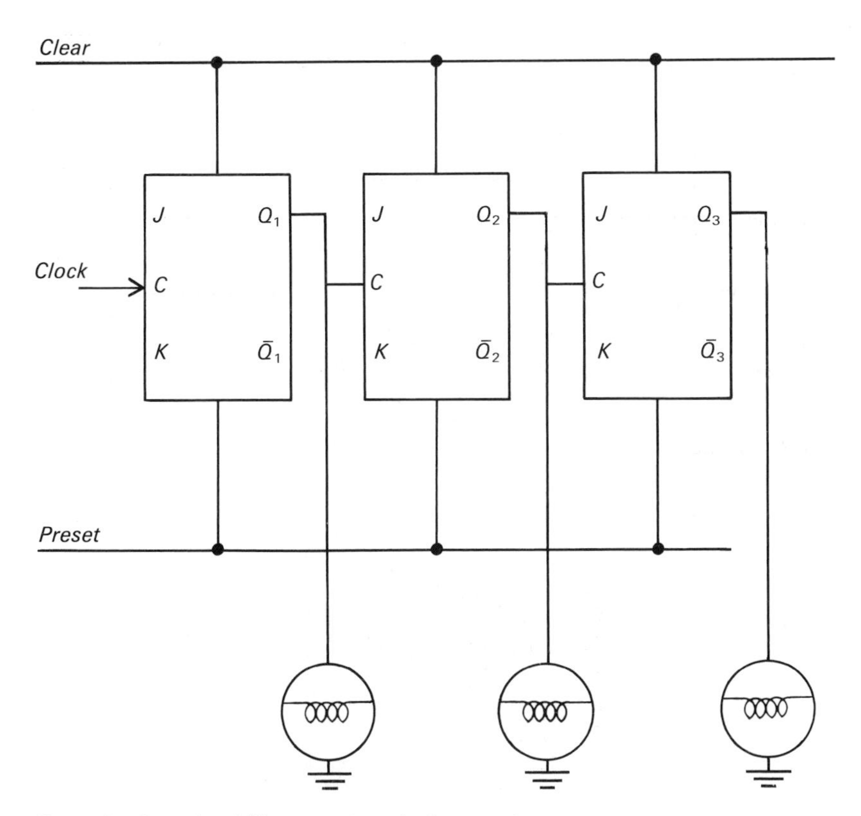

Fig. 6.5. A three-stage asynchronous binary up-counter.

Asynchronous binary up-counter

In an asynchronous counter, the trigger input of each bistable element is connected to the output of the preceeding element. Each flip flop acts as a 'divide by two' element and its output is delayed by a time Δt from its input. Thus the propagation delay increases with the number of stages. Figure 6.5 shows the circuit diagram and Fig. 6.6 the timing diagram for an asynchronous binary up-counter.

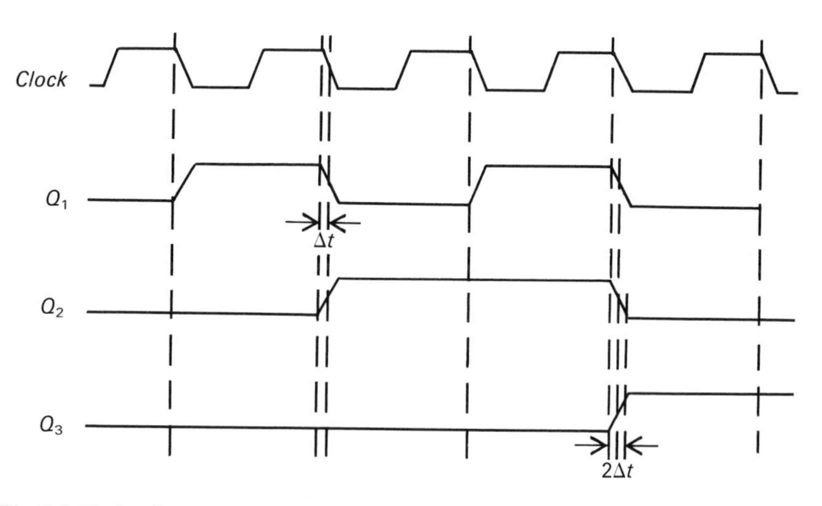

Fig. 6.6. Timing diagram for asynchronous binary up-counter.

The initial conditions for a binary up counter are *Clear* = 0 and *Preset* = 1, which sets all the outputs to 0. The counter will count pulses applied to the clock input when clear is set to 1.

Asynchronous binary down-counter

An asynchronous binary down-counter has the same properties as the up-counter. The circuit is shown in Fig. 6.7, and the timing diagram in Fig. 6.8.

This counter counts down from its maximum (all outputs equal to 1) to zero and is reset to maximum on the next falling edge of a clock pulse. The initial condition, to set all outputs to 1 is *Clear* = 1 *Preset* = 0. The counter will start counting when *Preset* is set to 1.

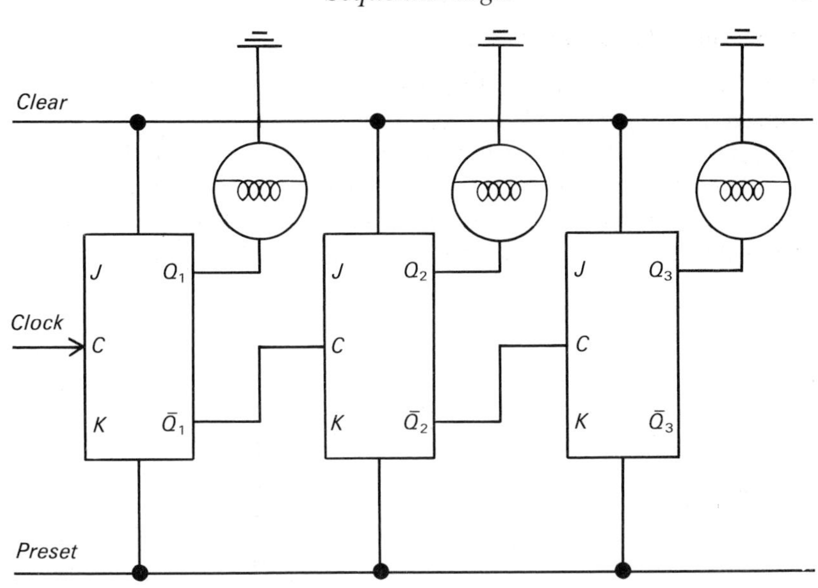

Fig. 6.7. Asynchronous binary down-counter.

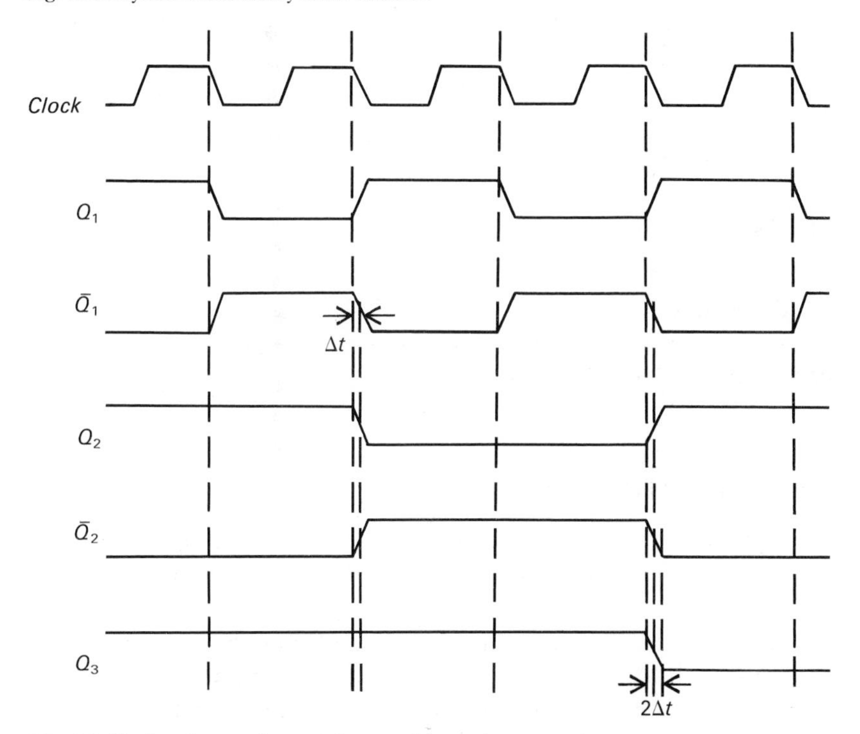

Fig. 6.8. Timing diagram for asynchronous binary down-counter.

Synchronous binary up-counter

The delay inherent in ripple through counters is avoided in synchronous counters by using the outputs of bistable circuits as gating signals to count pulses which are fed to all bistables in the counter. In this way all

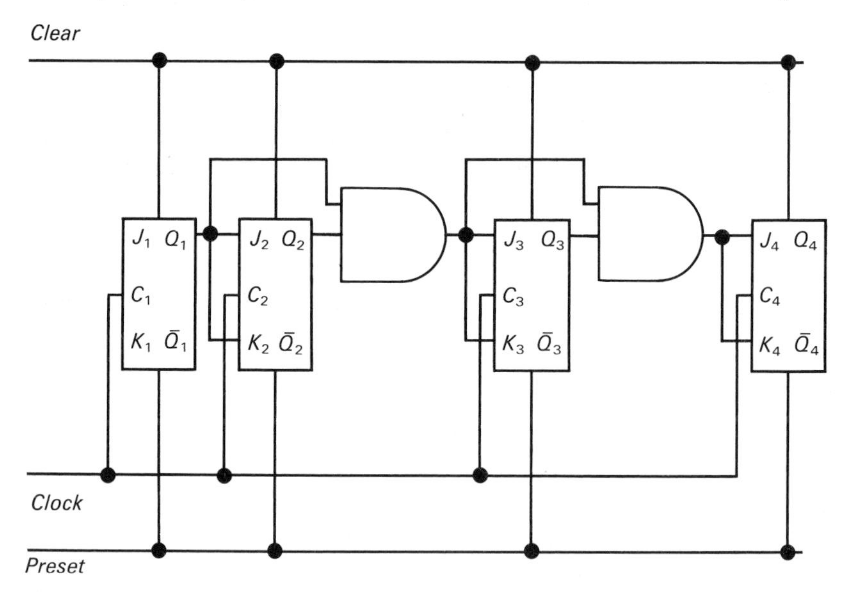

Fig. 6.9. A three-stage synchronous binary up-counter.

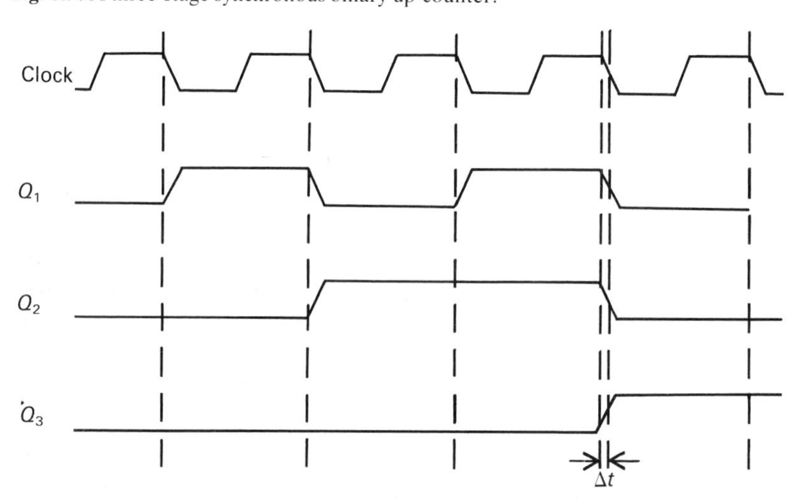

Fig. 6.10. Timing diagram for a three-stage synchronous binary up-counter.

stages that are required to change state on the arrival of the next clock pulse, do so simultaneously.

The circuit diagram for a three-stage synchronous binary up-counter is given in Fig. 6.9 and its timing diagram in Fig. 6.10. Note that the propagation delay Δt does not increase with the number of stages.

Synchronous binary down-counter

The above circuit diagram for the synchronous binary up-counter can be converted to a synchronous binary down-counter by changing the connections from one bistable to the next from the Q to the $\bar{Q}$ outputs. The output signals are still derived from the outputs.

The Initial conditions for synchronous counters are:
Preset = 0 *Clear* = 1 giving all outputs equal to 1, the initial condition for the down counter, and
Preset = 1 *Clear* = 0 giving all outputs equal to 0, the initial condition for the up counter.

For either counter to operate both *Clear* and *Preset* have to be set to 1.

Other types of counters

Counting in codes other than pure binary, for example Gray Code or a weighted code such as 1242BCD, in which only one bit changes at a time is achieved by gating between the stages of the counter. The form of the gating depends on the code being used.

6.4 MEMORIES AND REGISTERS

Both computer memories and registers (a single memory location in the Central Processor) store information in a defined number of bits. When information is written to or read from a register or a memory location the transfer is performed in parallel. In other words all the bits are transferred simultaneously along parallel connections known as a bus. In the central processor of a computer there are many registers each of which has its inputs fed from, and its outputs connected to a common bus (cf. Fig. 6.11).

If the registers each hold 8 bits of data then the parallel bus will consist of eight wires joining all corresponding inputs and outputs. In Section 6.2 '1-Bit Store Characteristics' the 1-bit store characteristics of the J-K Bistable were described and it is by using J-K's in this way that a

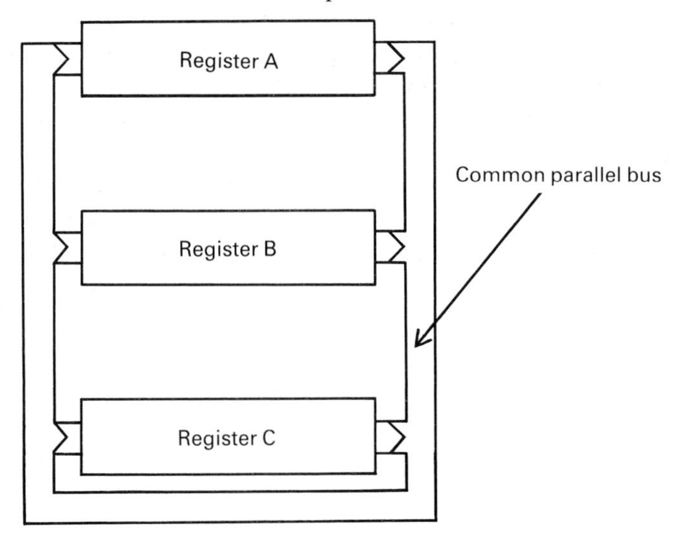

Fig. 6.11. Registers and a common parallel bus.

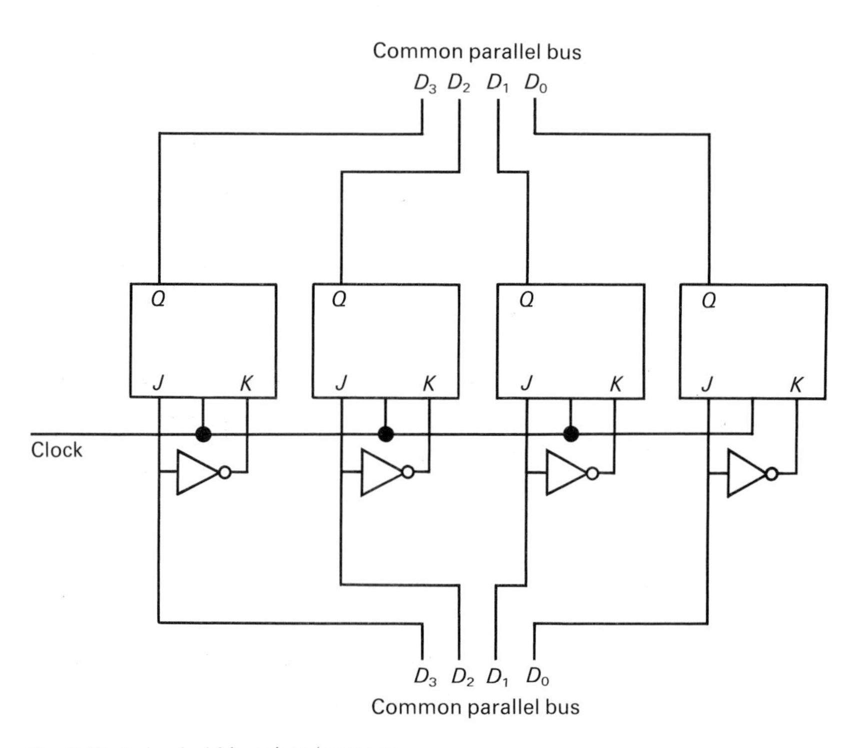

Fig. 6.12. A simple 4-bit register/memory.

register can be produced. Figure 6.12 shows how four J-K Bistables can be used to produce a 4-bit store or register, each bistable storing 1 bit.

Any inputs from the common parallel bus will be stored in the J-K Bistables on the falling edge of the clock pulse and will appear at the outputs to the common bus. For the system illustrated in Fig. 6.11 it must be possible to transfer data from one register to another via the parallel bus without affecting the third register. A method for selecting both which register is putting data onto the bus and for selecting which one is receiving the data from it must therefore be developed.

Since the register only reads data from the bus on the falling edge of the clock pulse, if the clock is fed to the register via a two-input AND gate, the register will only receive the clock signal when the other input

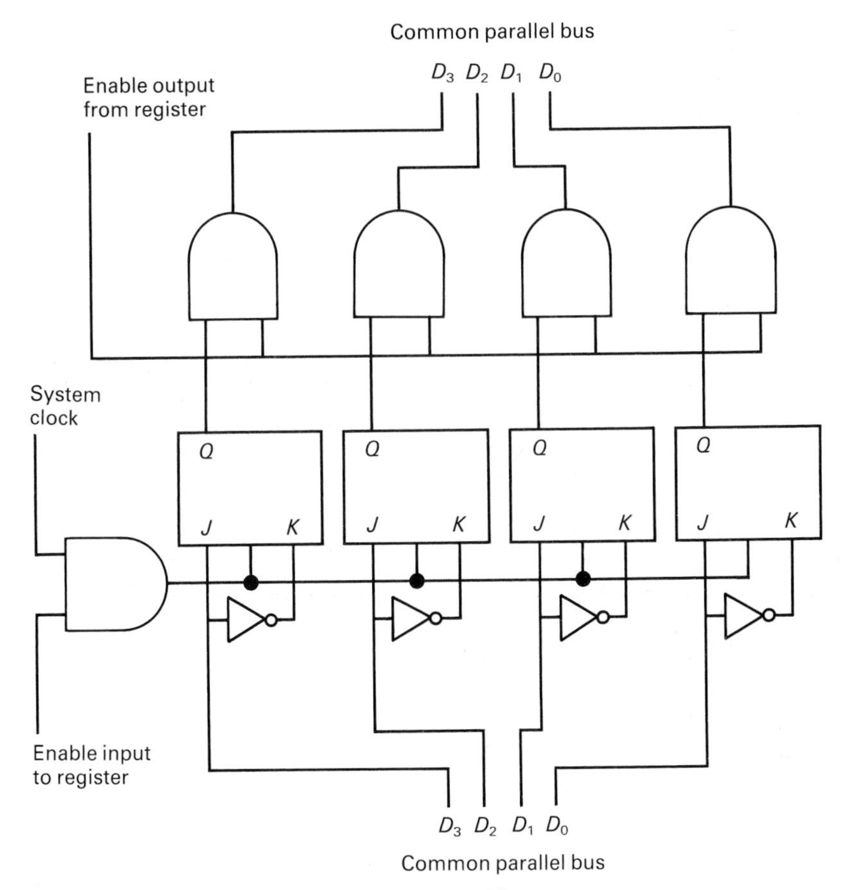

Fig. 6.13. A 4-bit register with input and output enable.

to the AND gate is a 1. The second signal to the AND gate is known as the input enable of the register (cf. Fig. 6.13).

Similarly the individual outputs could each be fed onto the common bus via a two-input AND gate and the second inputs to these gates would be the output enable of the register (cf. Fig. 6.14).

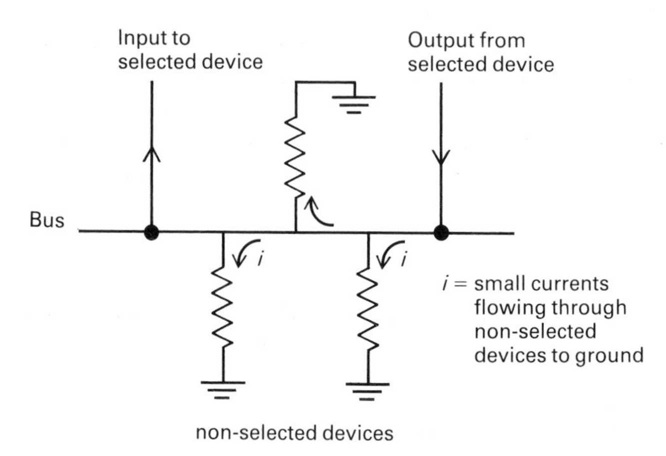

Fig. 6.14. Connections to a bus.

6.5 TRI-STATE LOGIC

A single bus line can have many devices connected to it. If each of these devices uses standard transistor/transistor logic they can effectively be considered as being a resistance connected to ground when viewed from the bus line. When a logical 1 (+5 volts) is being transferred from one device to another via the bus the effect of each of the other non-selected

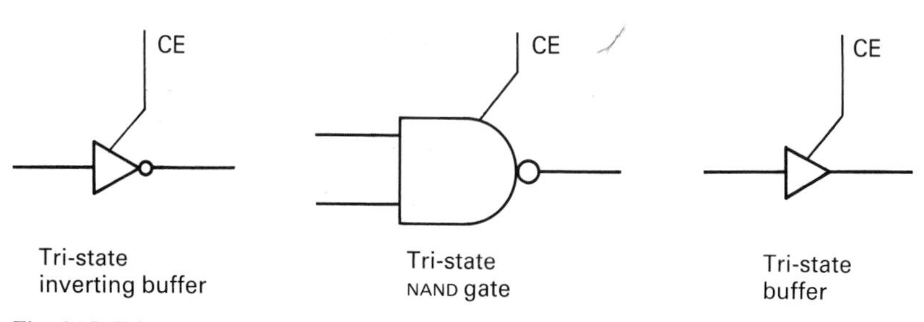

Fig. 6.15. Tri-state devices.

devices would be to conduct a small current which pulls down the signal and can effect the input to the selected device.

To overcome these effects tri-state logic must be introduced. Tri-state gates have three outputs, high, low and open circuit. The third state effectively disconnects the device from its output. Figure 6.15 shows some tri-state devices.

A tri-state device has a chip enable input. When this is a 1 the gate acts in the normal TTL way. When it is 0 the gate is in its third state which means that it is seen as being disconnected.

Tri-state buffers are used on the outputs of most devices. Figure 6.16 shows their use on the outputs of a register or memory.

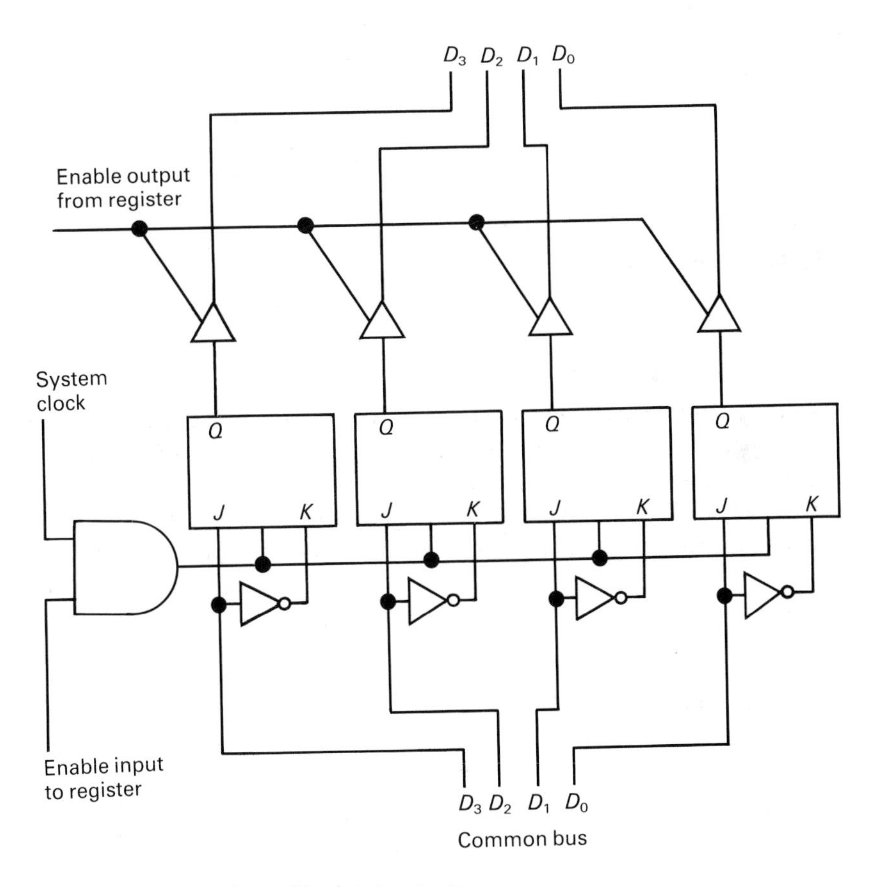

Fig. 6.16. A 4-bit register with tri-state outputs.

6.6 OTHER TYPES OF BISTABLES

The R-S Bistable

The R-S Bistable has two inputs, Set (S) and Reset (R) and an output Q as shown in Fig. 6.17.

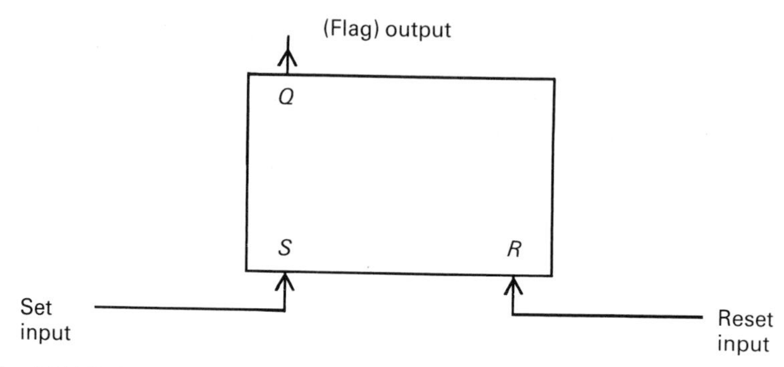

Fig. 6.17. The R-S Bistable.

The output is set (takes up a logical 1) when a signal is applied to the S input and will stay set when the input is removed. The output is reset, (goes to a logical 0) when a 1 is applied to the R input and stays 0 when the reset signal is removed.

This device is commonly used as a flag both in a processor and in input output. Consider a printer connected to a processor as shown in Fig. 6.18.

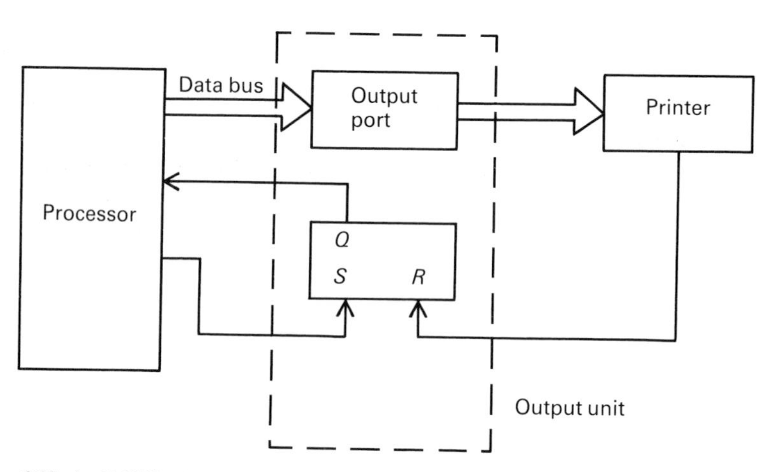

Fig. 6.18. An R-S Bistable used as a flag.

When the processor wants to print a character it first checks the status flag (the R-S Bistable) to see if the printer is free. If the flag is clear the processor transmits a character and sets the flag indicating that the printer is busy. When the character has been printed the flag is cleared by the printer resetting the bistable.

The D-type Bistable

The characteristics of the *D*-type Bistable (Fig. 6.19) are similar to those of the J-K Flip Flop. The inputs *Clear* and *Preset* are active low and are used to set the outputs in the same way as those of the J-K Bistable. With both *Clear* and *Preset* set to 1 the input *D* is stored on the rising edge of the clock pulse.

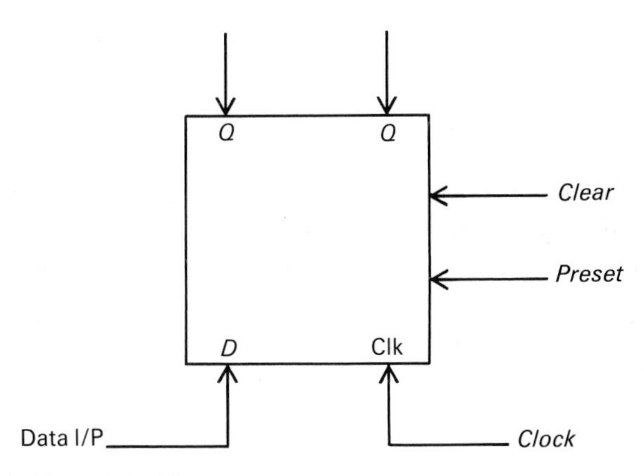

Fig. 6.19. The *D*-type Bistable.

The *D*-type Bistable is used in much the same way as the J-K in building registers and counters.

The following chapter describes the basic structure of a computer and illustrates its characteristics by considering a simple machine consisting of the circuits described in this and previous chapters.

Chapter 7

The Operation of a Central Processor

7.1 INTRODUCTION

This chapter describes the hardware configuration of a simple computer system. The storage and execution of machine code instructions is explained to give an overview of the operation of a central processor.

7.2 MACHINE CODE INSTRUCTION FORMAT

The instructions which a computer executes are held in the computer's memory and called machine code. A program written in any programming language has to be converted to machine code before it can be executed. This conversion is performed by one of three types of systems programs, a compiler, an interpreter or an assembler.

The basic structure of any microcomputer system is a processor connected to various support devices by three buses, the control bus, the address bus and the data bus. (cf. Fig. 7.1). The processor contains registers. Machine code instructions operate on data held in these registers or transfer data or instructions, in parallel, between the registers and memory using the buses.

An instruction will be held in memory as a binary pattern which must specify the operation to be performed, the source or sources of the data and the destination of the result. For example, *Add the contents of memory address 100 to the contents of address 207 and store the result in address 365*. The sources and destinations are either registers or memory locations. The number of sources will depend on the instruction, those such as Add or Subtract will require two sources whilst others like Shift or Complement will need only one.

Since computer memories are large, ranging from tens of thousands, to millions of addresses, an instruction format containing all of these components would be very long. Their lengths are kept short by a combination of the techniques:

(i) making the destination the same as one of the sources;

(ii) making one of the sources and the destination implicit rather than explicit; and

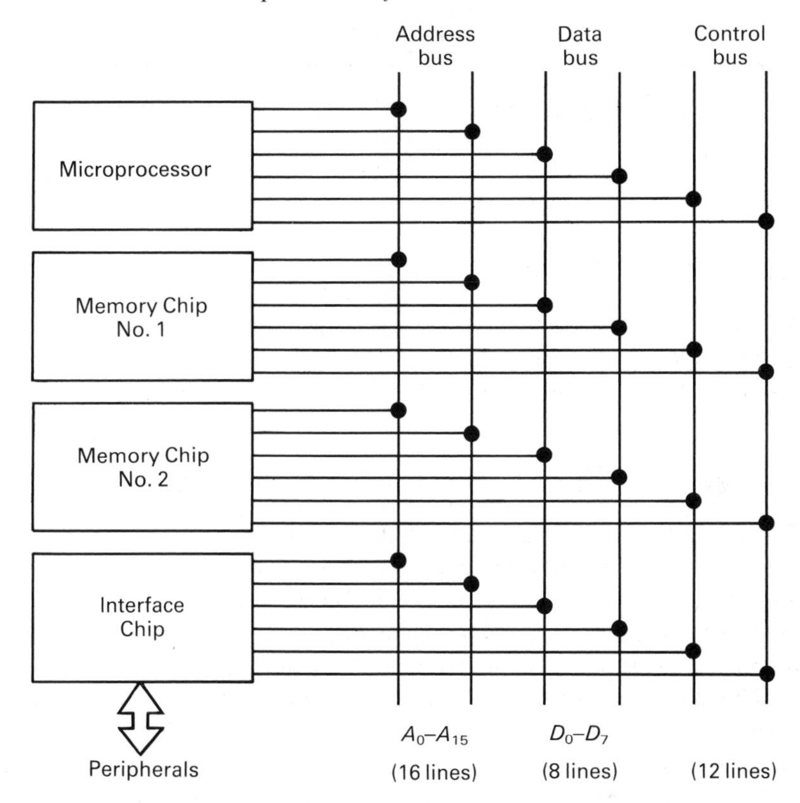

Fig. 7.1. Bus structure for an 8-bit microcomputer.

(iii) limiting addresses to be registers or their contents.

Many computers use instructions which have a register as combined source and destination. For example, ADDA 20_{16} adds the contents of memory address 20_{16} to the contents of register A leaving the result in register A. These types of instructions are stored in a binary format consisting of an operation (e.g. ADDA) and an operand (20_{16}) (cf. Fig. 7.2).

ADDA	20
Operation	Operand
00011011	00100000

Fig. 7.2. The format of a one address instruction.

Computers can be organized on either a word basis or a byte basis. Usually on a word-based system the whole of an instruction will be transferred from memory to the instruction register at one time. Whilst on a byte-based system one transfer will be needed to obtain the operation code and another one or two to get the operand.

7.3 MACHINE CODE INSTRUCTION SET

Machine code is specific to a processor and is established during its design. However, the instruction set can be categorized into four main groups.

(i) Data manipulation instructions; to perform arithmetic and logical operations and to compare their results against expected values.

(ii) Data transfer instructions; to transfer information between registers, between registers and memory, and between registers or memory and input output devices.

(iii) Program manipulation instructions; to perform both conditional and unconditional jumps and to handle subroutines.

(iv) Status management instructions; to manipulate the various flags in the status register.

7.4 A SIMPLE WORD-BASED COMPUTER SYSTEM

The following sections use a simple word-based computer system firstly to illustrate some of the functions performed by processor registers and secondly to explain how the sequence of events required to execute a machine code instruction are generated. Figure 7.3 shows the layout of a simple word-based computer and its connection to an external memory.

Processor registers

Registers are the key to a central processor's architecture, the characteristics and performance of a processor being determined to a large extent by the number, length and functions of its registers. Figure 7.3 shows a typical register set for a small computer. It should be noted that a register may have its output directed to one of a number of internal buses by means of separate enable signals.

The program counter contains the address in memory of the next instruction. The instruction cycle starts by placing the address from the

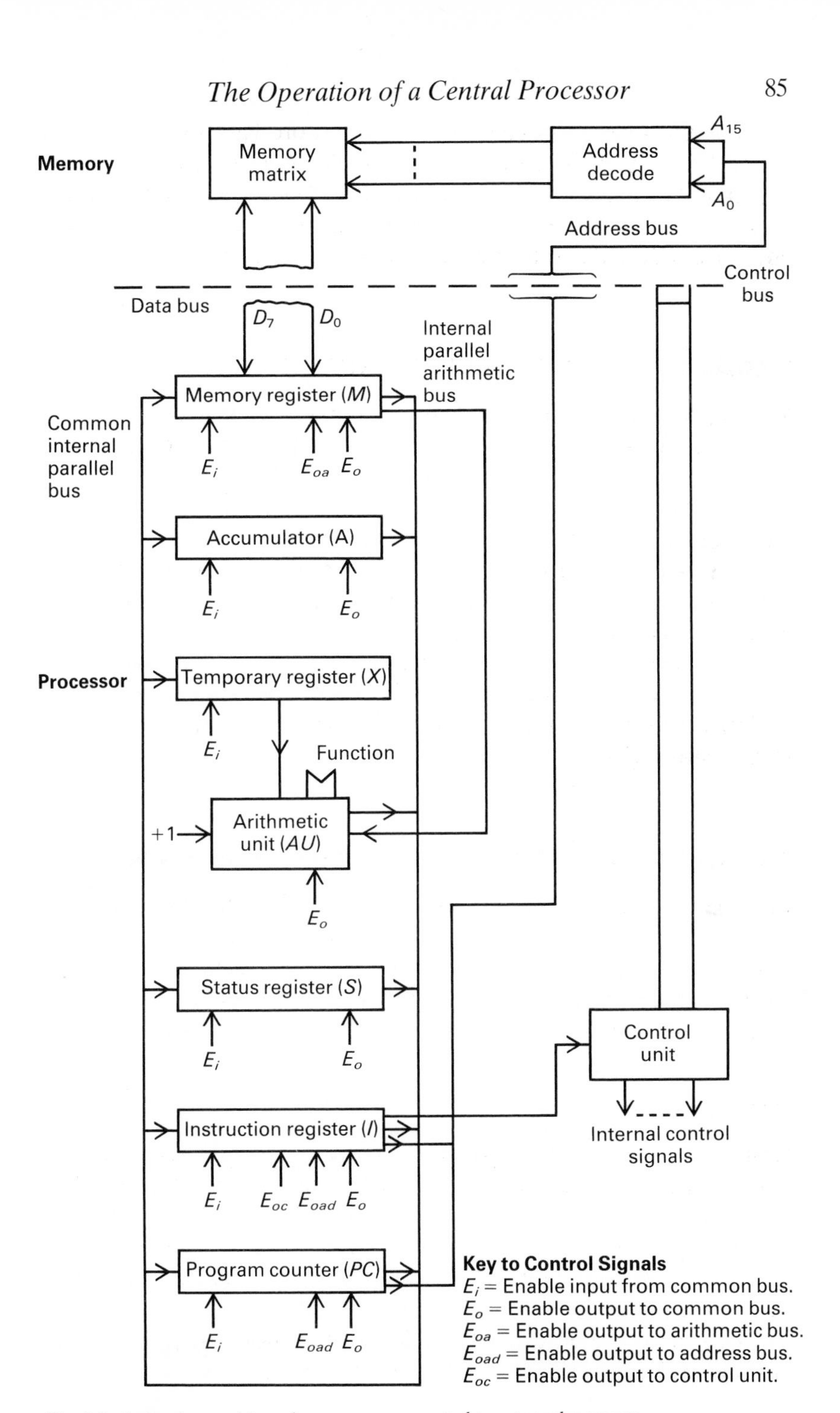

Fig. 7.3. A simple word-based processor connected to external memory.

program counter onto the address bus in order to obtain the instruction from memory.

On a word-based system the processor increments the program counter so that the next instruction cycle will fetch the next instruction. On a byte-based system, however, if the instruction occupies more than 1 byte of memory, the program counter must be incremented each time a byte is read.

The instruction register holds the current instruction until it is decoded. The bit length of this register is equal to the bit length of the basic instructions. Some processors have two instruction registers, enabling them to obtain the next instruction whilst executing the current one, a technique known as pipelining.

The accumulator or A register is the main storage register of the CPU. Most computers have several accumulators.

The memory register is the register to and from which memory transfers take place.

The temporary register (X) is a register used to hold one of the operands during arithmetic operations. The second operand is presented to the arithmetic unit from another register via the internal arithmetic bus.

The status register holds a number of 1-bit flags that indicate the state of conditions inside the CPU. These flags form the basis of all computer decision-making since their state can be examined and a program jump made depending on the result.

Different computers have different combinations of flags, the most common ones being:

(i) The carry flag which when set to 1 indicates that the last operation generated a carry from the most significant bit.

(ii) The zero flag, a 1 in which signifies that the result of the last operation was zero.

(iii) The overflow flag, a 1 indicating that the last operation resulted in two's complement overflow. (The result being too large to be stored).

(iv) The sign flag, which when set to 1 indicates that the most significant bit of the result of the last operation was a 1 (i.e. a negative number in two's complement form).

Instruction cycles

The instruction cycle consists of two parts, the read cycle and the obey cycle.

The read cycle is common to all machine code instructions and is that part of the cycle in which the next instruction is obtained from the memory location specified in the program counter. The obey cycle is that part of the instruction cycle in which the sequence of steps necessary to execute the instruction which has just been read is performed.

A complete program is therefore, executed by a series of instruction cycles, as shown in Fig. 7.4.

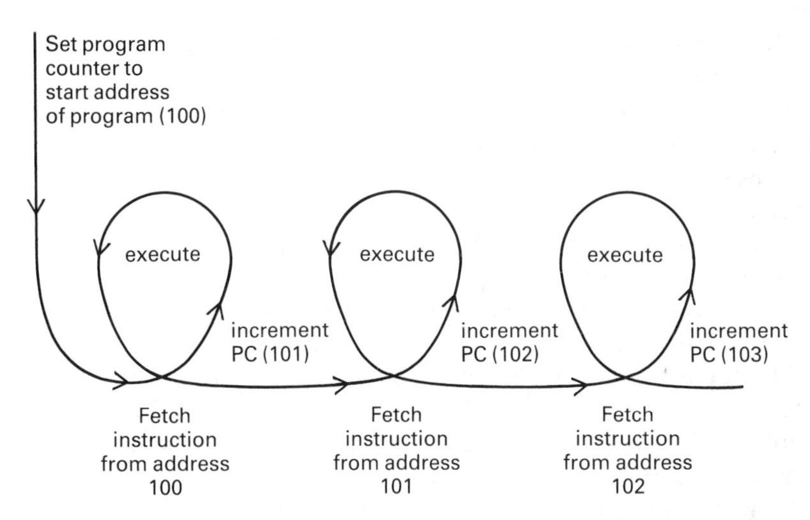

Fig. 7.4. The execution of a machine code program on a word-based computer system.

The control unit

An instruction cycle must, by definition, be made up of a sequence of steps to read and execute a particular instruction. It is the role of the control unit to generate this sequence of steps by providing the required internal control signals (enables) and the external signals on the control bus.

During the read cycle the binary pattern of the next machine code instruction in the program is read into the instruction register and the binary digits representing the required operation transferred to the control unit. This pattern can then be recognized and the required sequence of steps needed to execute the instruction (e.g. ADDA 20_{16}) performed (cf. Fig. 7.5).

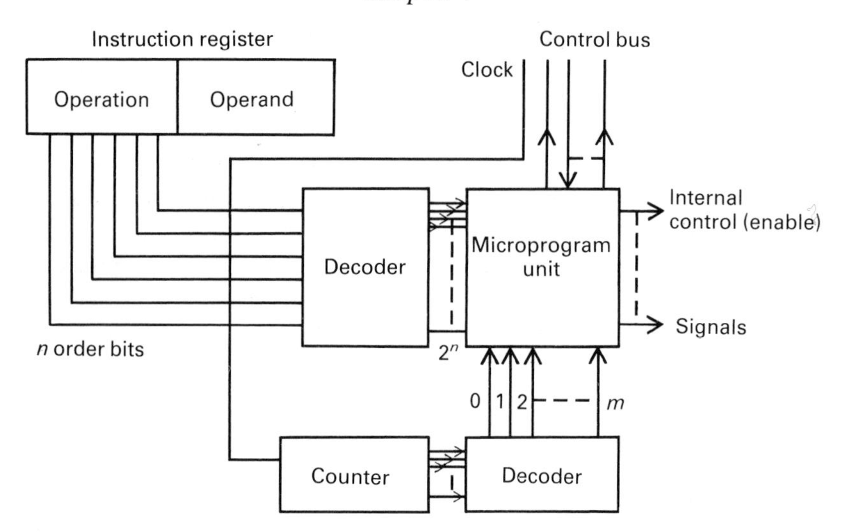

Fig. 7.5. Block diagram of a control unit.

The control unit consists of circuitry to generate the required sequence of steps for each machine code instruction. For the computer shown in Fig. 7.3, the sequence of control signals needed to perform the instruction '*Add the contents of the address specified to register A*' would be:

	Step	Operation
Read cycle	1	Output the contents of the program counter to the address bus (E_{oad} signal on program counter) *and* send a read signal to the memory via the control bus.
	2	Transfer the contents of the program counter to the X register (E_o program counter, E_i on X register) *and* gate +1 to the least significant stage of the arithmetic unit *and* add.
	3	Transfer the result from the arithmetic unit back to the program counter (E_o on arithmetic unit, E_i on program counter).
	4	Transfer the instruction from the memory register to the instruction register (E_o on memory register E_i on instruction register).
	5	Transfer the operation code for the instruction from the instruction register to the control unit (E_{oc} on the instruction register).

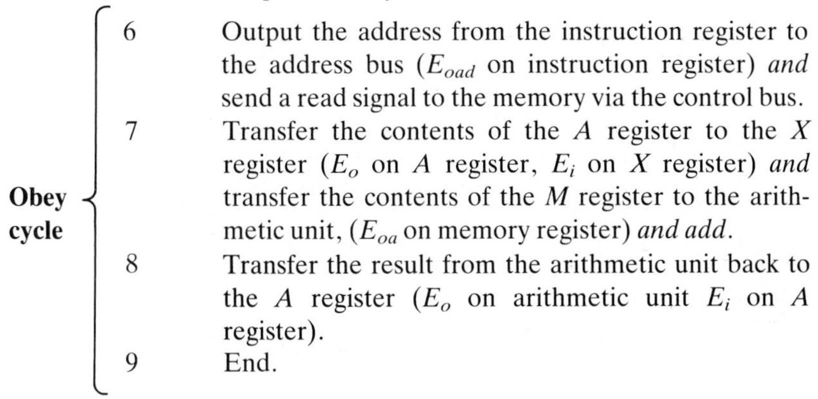

Obey cycle

6 Output the address from the instruction register to the address bus (E_{oad} on instruction register) *and* send a read signal to the memory via the control bus.

7 Transfer the contents of the A register to the X register (E_o on A register, E_i on X register) *and* transfer the contents of the M register to the arithmetic unit, (E_{oa} on memory register) *and add*.

8 Transfer the result from the arithmetic unit back to the A register (E_o on arithmetic unit E_i on A register).

9 End.

The sequence of steps needed to execute one machine code instruction is called a *microprogram* and each step is known as a *micro-instruction*. The individual control signals which make up each micro-instruction and which are executed simultaneously are called *micro-orders* and are the basic hardware operations of the computer.

In processor design, when microprograms have been written for each of the required machine code instructions every possible occurrence of each micro-order will have been defined and it can then be implemented in hardware. The sequencing within the control unit is controlled by the clock signal which when fed into a counter and decoder will give one active line for each clock pulse as shown in Fig. 7.6. These timing signals are used to control the processor.

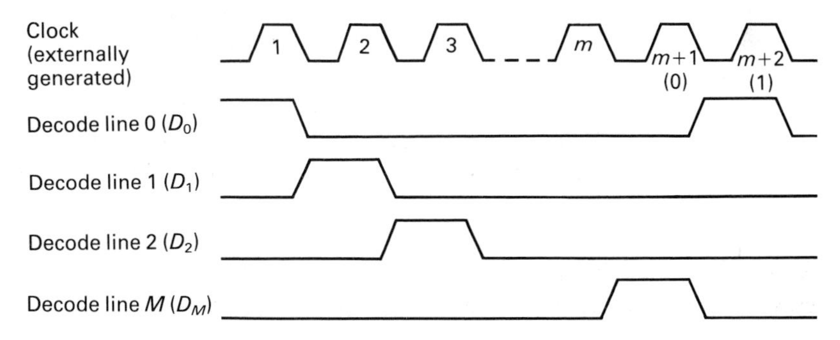

Fig. 7.6. Timing signals.

When the counter has reached its maximum value it returns to zero and the next instruction is started.

The read cycle is independent of the instruction to be executed and is totally determined by these timing signals. The obey cycle depends on the operation being performed and is determined by both the output of the operation code decoder and by the timing signals.

For the instruction ADDA the input enable to the *X* register has to be set to 1 at step 2 ($D_2=1$) and step 7 ($D_7=1$). Step 2 is part of the read cycle and is independent of the instruction being executed whilst step 7 is only valid for the ADDA instruction.

If the operation code for ADDA is 00011011 then after step 5 the twenty-seventh line from the operation code decoder will be set to 1, ($OP_{27}=1$) and the circuit shown in Fig. 7.7 can be used to generate the enable input to *X* register signal.

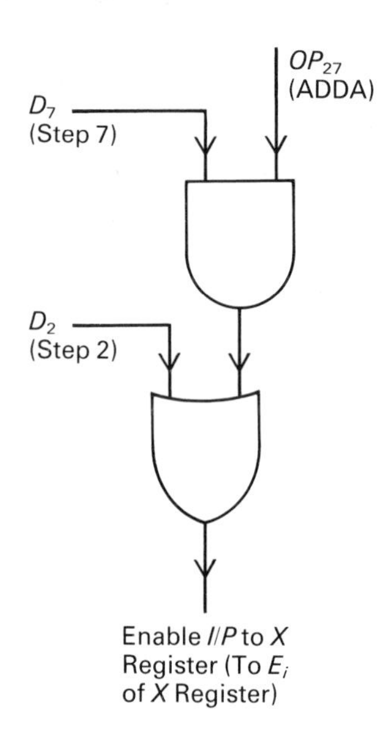

Fig. 7.7. Micro-order circuit for enable *I*/*P* to *X* register (ADDA only).

Other instructions will need the input to the *X* register to be enabled at other times and the circuit shown in Fig. 7.7 has to be extended to cater for all of them. In other words the micro-order enable *I*/*P* to the *X* register can be implemented in hardware as shown in Fig. 7.8.

Having written the microprograms, every micro-order can be implemented in hardware in a similar way irrespective of whether it is an internal signal or a signal for the external control bus (e.g. read memory) and in this way the control unit can be constructed.

This chapter has described the configuration and operation of a central processor. In the next chapter the connections and modes of operation used in interfacing a peripheral device to a processor are discussed.

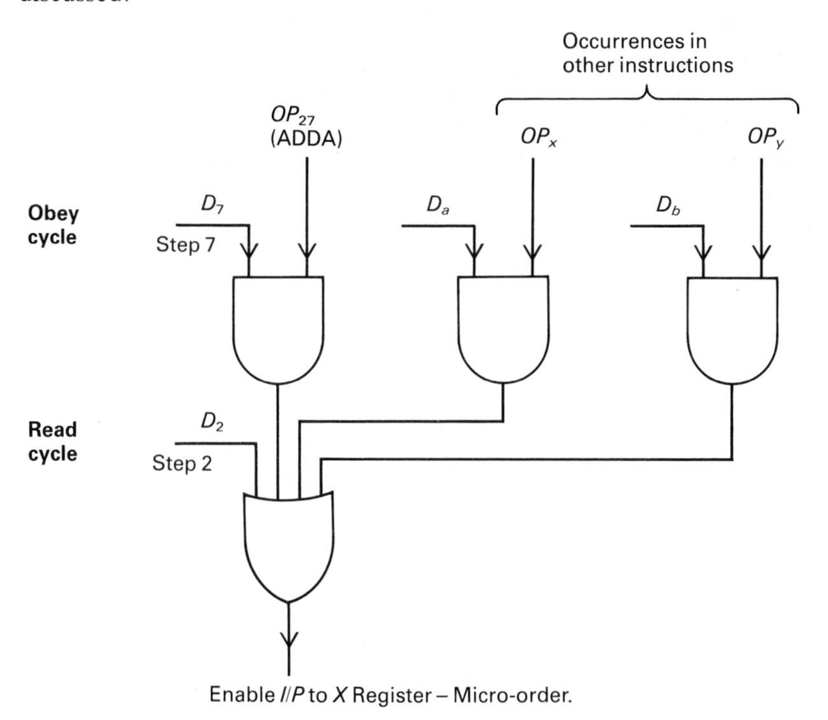

Fig. 7.8. Implementation of the micro-order enable I/P to X register.

Chapter 8

Interfacing

8.1 INTRODUCTION

This chapter describes the two basic techniques used in transferring data between a processor and its peripherals. Information is transmitted to, or received from, a peripheral by the processor a byte at a time on its data bus. This bus is connected to the peripheral via an interface which is the circuitry linking the data bus with the cable to the device.

There are two basic types of interface, a parallel interface in which each bit of the byte representing a character is transmitted simultaneously down eight separate wires in the cable, and a serial interface in which the 8 bits are sent one after the other down a single wire.

Serial interfaces are used to connect relatively slow devices, such as visual display units, which may be remote from the processor. Parallel interfaces are, however, used for faster peripherals which are usually located nearer to the processor and which require higher data transfer rates.

8.2 PARALLEL INTERFACES

A parallel interface is used to convert data to the required signal levels and to hold it for a long enough period for either the peripheral or the processor to read it, depending on the direction of the transfer.

An example of a parallel interface is given in Fig. 8.1.

Parallel output port

A parallel output port in its simplest form is a parallel register, as described in Chapter 6, with the addition of 2 bits which may be used to control the transfer. A circuit diagram for an output port is shown in Fig. 8.2 (see p. 94).

The normal method used to control the timing of all transfers is known as *handshaking*. When the processor is transferring information to the peripheral it first checks the *Busy* line to see if the device is available. If this is clear, i.e. the device is available, it loads a new

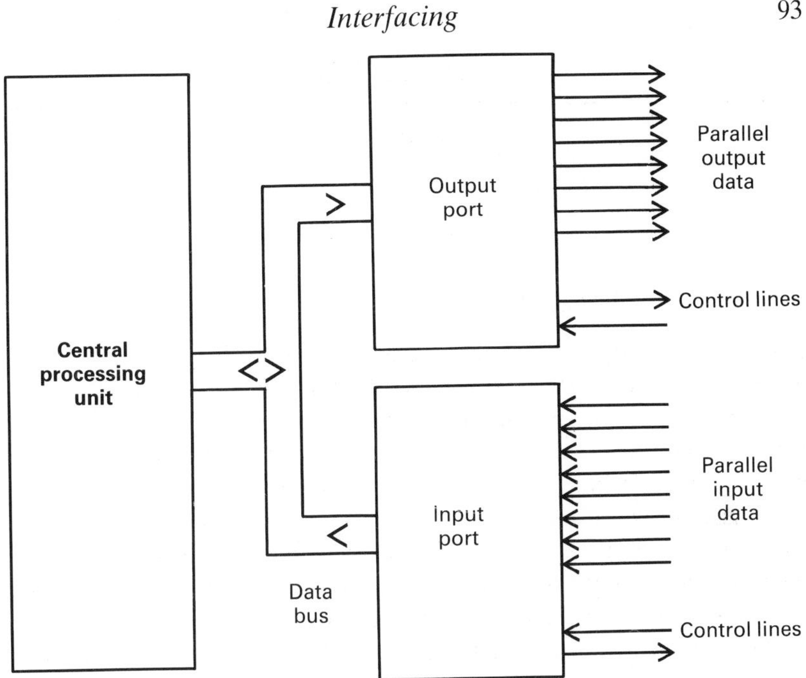

Fig. 8.1. A parallel interface.

character into the interface setting the *strobe* line to activate the peripheral. The peripheral then sets the *Busy* line while it is handling the data so that it stops further data from being sent. When the current data has been handled the *Busy* line is cleared by the peripheral. The processor detects that it has been cleared and loads the next character into the interface. This sequence continues until the processor has run out of data to send.

Using this technique, a typical microcomputer can transmit data at rates reaching 50,000 characters/second. This is faster than most peripheral devices can handle and provides a reliable method for transmission over short distances.

Parallel input port

An 8-bit parallel input port with control lines is shown in Fig. 8.3.

The handshaking lines for this port are used in a similar way to those of the output port.

When the peripheral sends data to the port it sets the *Busy* line for a short period latching the output (X) to a 1. A program running in the

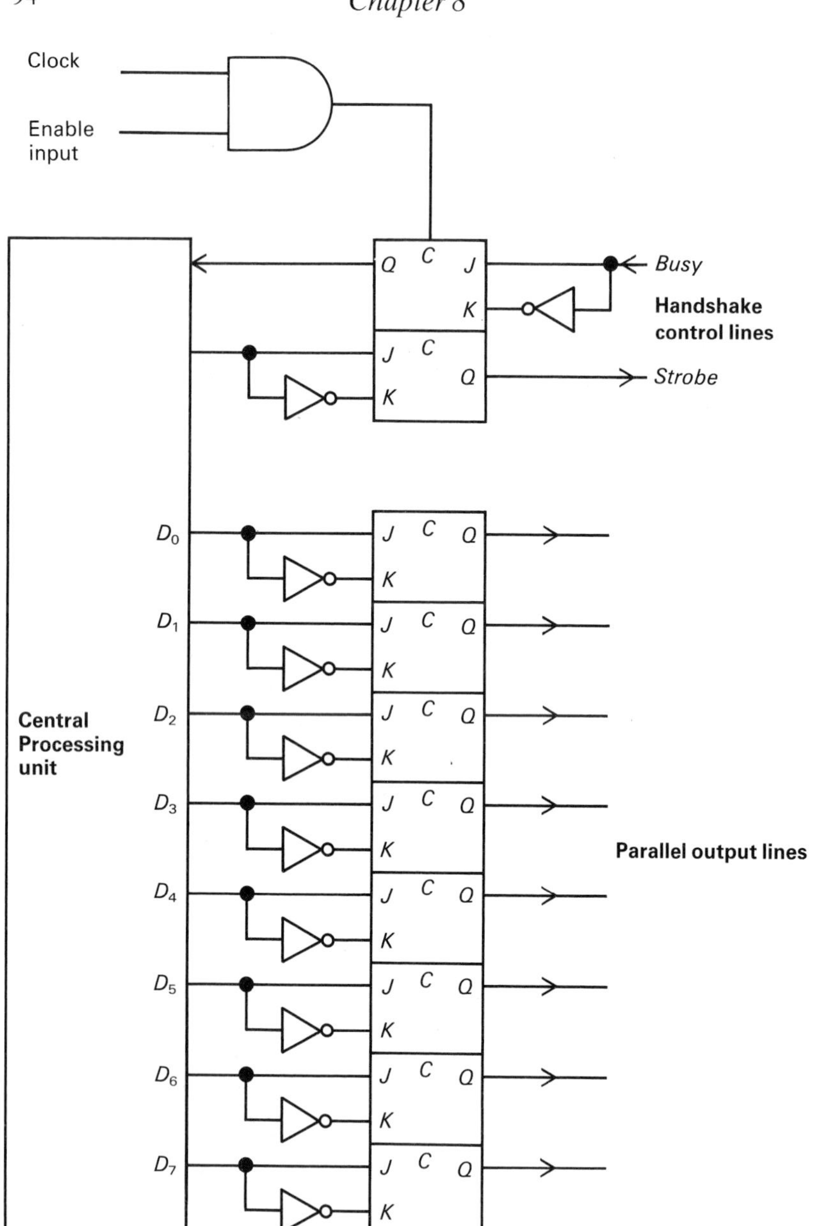

Fig. 8.2. A parallel output port.

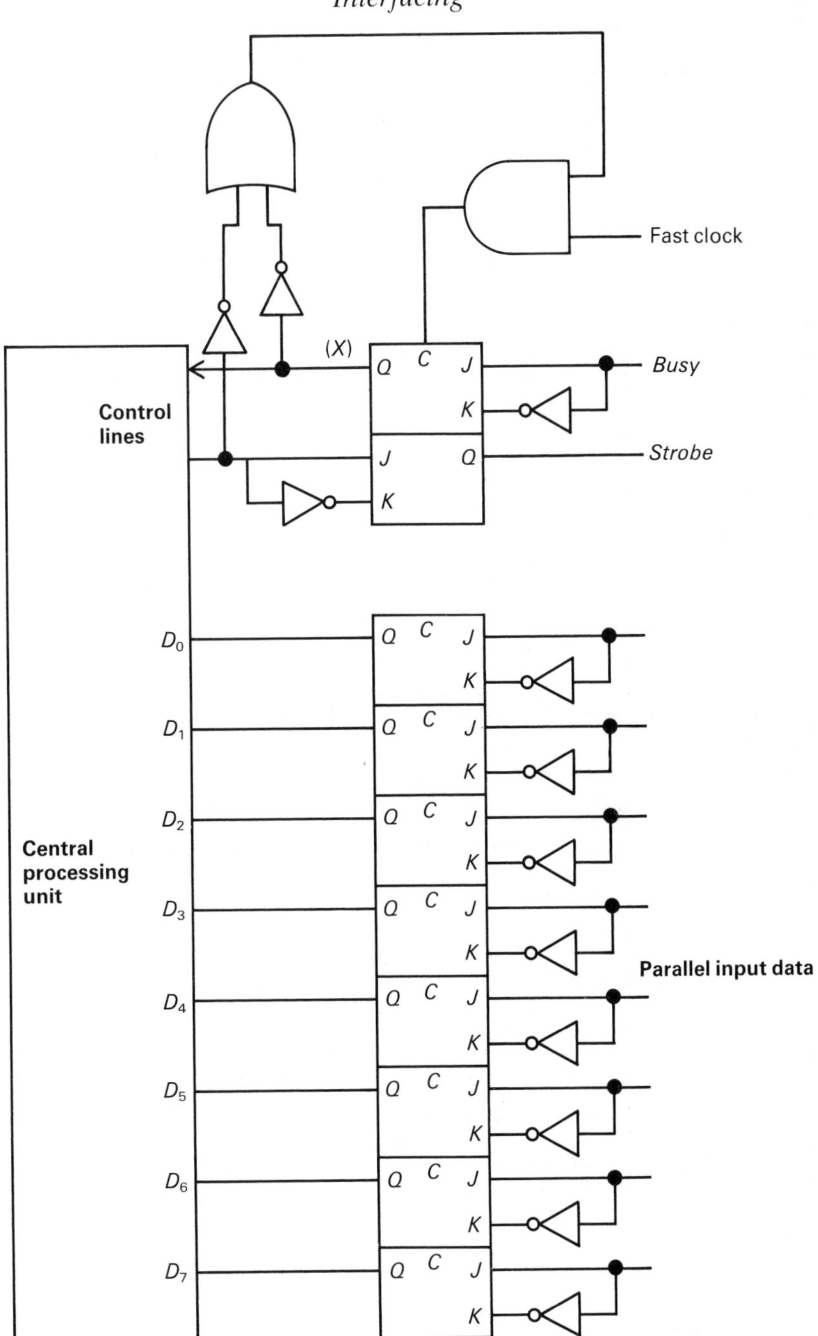

Fig. 8.3. A parallel input port.

processor detects that the busy line is set and reads the data at the same time indicating to the peripheral that it is doing so by setting the strobe line to 1, which clears the busy line latch. The program then resets the strobe line indicating to the peripheral that it is free to send more data.

In microcomputer systems these ports are often combined and a discussion of currently available parallel interface chips is included in the next chapter.

8.3 SERIAL INTERFACES

For input a serial interface is used to convert data received from a peripheral in serial form to parallel form for input to the data bus. On output, it converts data received from the data bus into serial form for transmission to a similar interface in the peripheral.

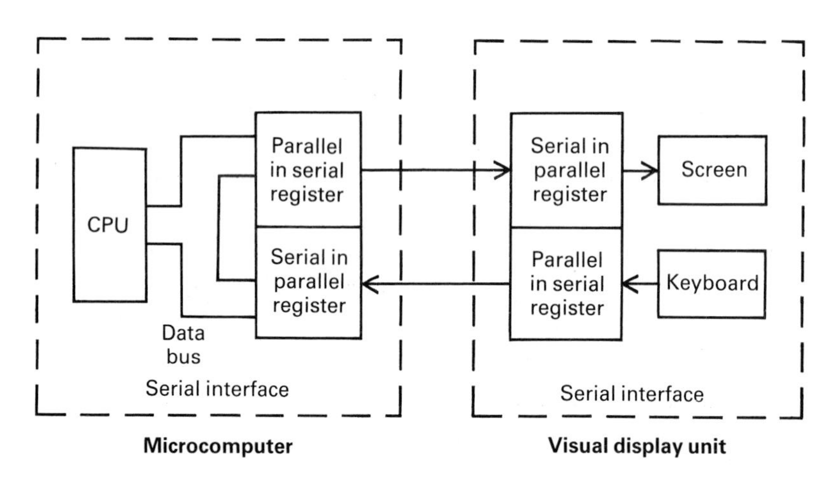

Fig. 8.4. Serial transmission to a VDU.

There are two basic types of interfaces, asynchronous and synchronous, described later, both of which are implemented in LSI technology, and both of which use serial-in-parallel and parallel-in-serial registers.

A serial-to-parallel register

A Serial-In-Parallel-Out register (SIPO) reads data in serial form, in phase with the clock pulse, and converts it to parallel form for output.

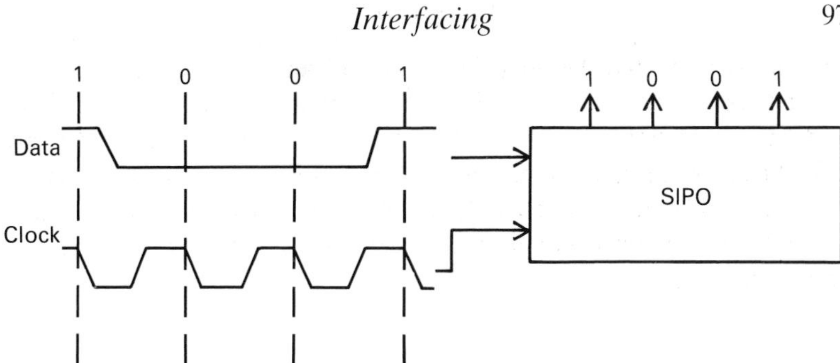

Fig. 8.5. A SIPO.

Figure 8.5 shows a SIPO (or forward shifting register which samples the incoming data line on the falling edge of the clock pulse and which can be designed from J-K Bistables (Fig. 8.6).

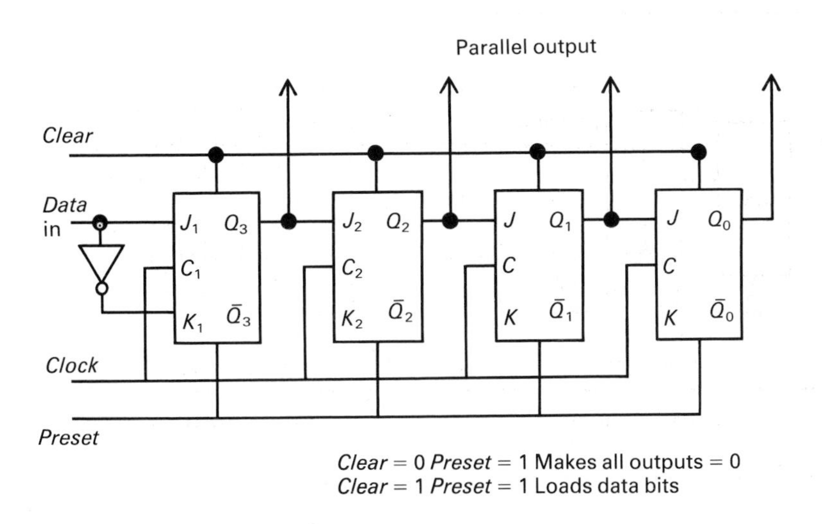

Fig. 8.6. Circuit diagram for a SIPO.

The operation of this circuit is summarized by the timing diagram shown in Fig. 8.7.

For the circuit shown in Fig. 8.6, four clock pulses are needed to read in 4 bits of serial data and for them to be shifted into the appropriate bit of the parallel output. The clock must be stopped after four cycles to freeze the output and stop further data from being read.

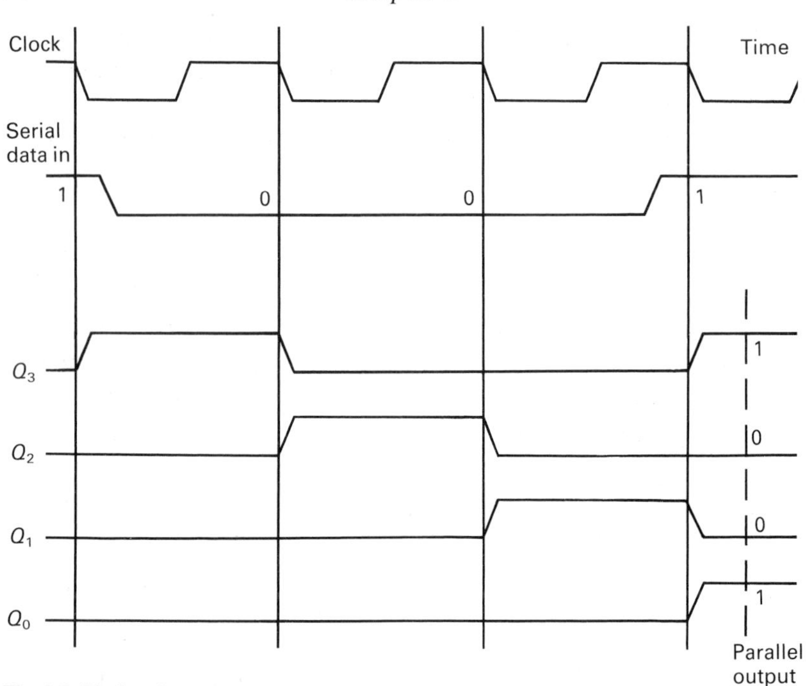

Fig. 8.7. Timing diagram for a SIPO.

A parallel-in-serial register

A Parallel-In-Serial-Out register (PISO) reads data on receipt of a load signal and uses the clock to transmit this in serial form down a single line at a given rate which depends on the clock frequency.

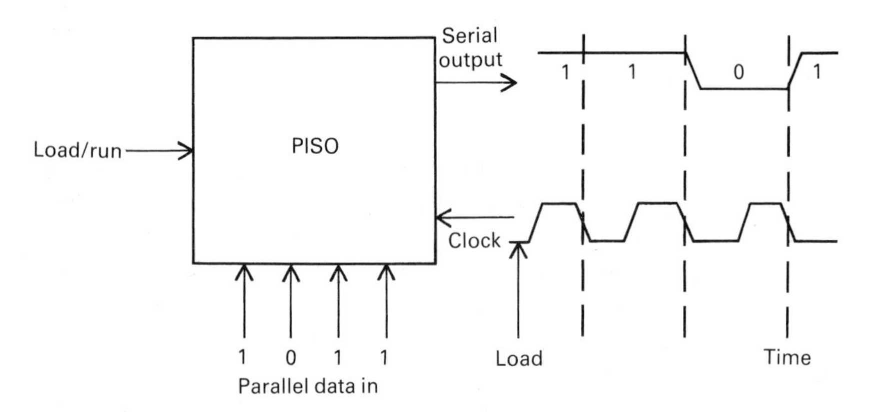

Fig. 8.8. A PISO.

Figure 8.8 shows a PISO which loads data from the parallel inputs when the load/run line is a 1 and transmits each bit on the falling edge of the clock pulse which is enabled when the run/load line goes to 0. This circuit can be designed from J-K Bistables and its implementation is shown in Fig. 8.9.

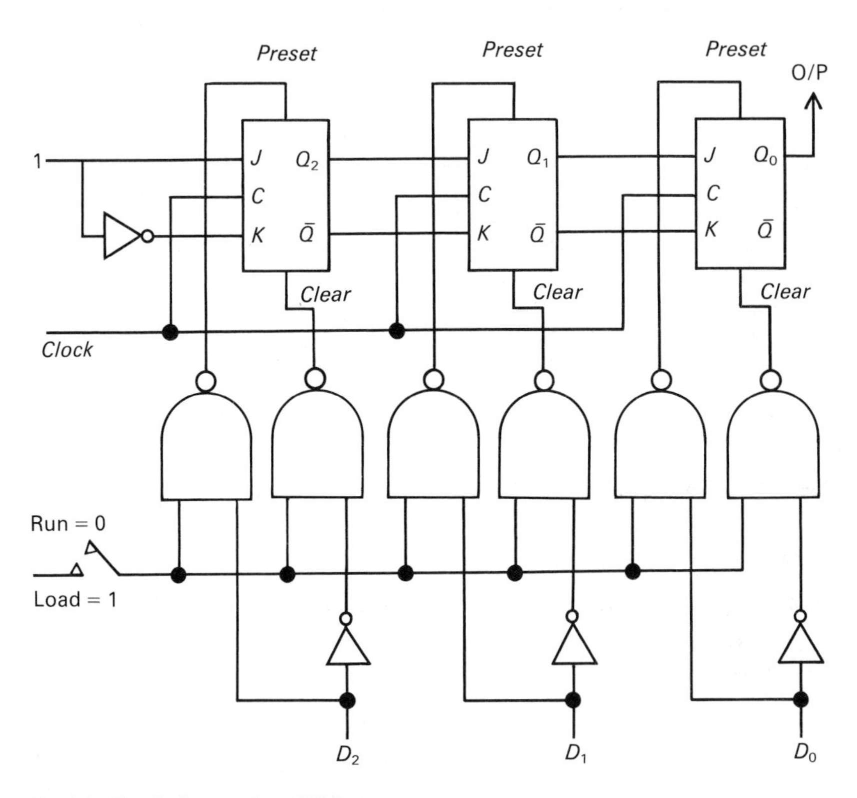

Fig. 8.9. Circuit diagram for a PISO.

With the load/run switch set to 1 the parallel input data, $D_2D_1D_0$ is loaded into the J-K Bistables using the *Clear* and *Preset* inputs. When the switch is set to 0, the inputs to each *Clear* and *Preset* are set to 1 and the data is shifted one place to the right on each falling edge of the clock pulse. The values on the J and K inputs of the first stage make the output line, taken from the Q output of the third stage, go to a 1 after the 3 data bits have been transmitted.

Figure 8.10 shows the timing diagram for this circuit being loaded with, and transmitting, the binary pattern 010.

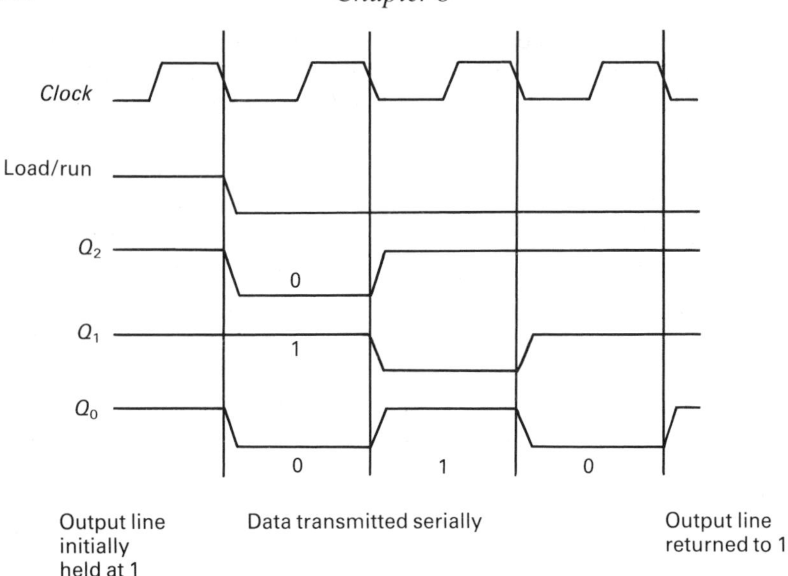

Fig. 8.10

Asynchronous serial data transfer

The ASCII character for the letter A with *even* parity is:

0 100 000 1

Parity bit (↑ under the first 0) — Least significant bit (↑ under the final 1)

To receive data from a peripheral, the interface at the processor must be able to detect when data is being sent, since characters can be received by the interface at any time. This is known as *asynchronous* data transfer. For example, for a VDU the time at which the keys are pressed depends only on the operator and is not synchronized in any way to the timing within the computer system.

The interface at the computer must, therefore, detect when a new character is being sent. To achieve this, the interconnecting line is normally held at a 1 level when no information is being transferred, and a *start* bit of level 0 is sent before the 8 bits of the character itself. The interface now has a clear change from a 1 to 0 on the incoming line to inform it that a character is being sent.

The interface must then sample each of the data bits and must, therefore, know for how long each bit is going to be on the line before the next is transmitted. The duration of each bit depends on the clock frequency, a characteristic known in data transmission as the *baud rate*.

In this case it is equivalent to the number of bits per second that are being sent. The computer and peripheral interfaces must both be set to the same *baud rate* before the system will work correctly. There are a limited number of standard rates that have been agreed internationally, and these are 110, 300, 600, 1200, 2400, 4800, and 9600 baud.

Once the *baud rate* has been set, the length of time that each pulse is on the line is fixed for example, at 300 baud each bit has a duration of 3.3 milliseconds (3.3×10^{-3} seconds). As soon as this start bit has been received the receiving interface circuit looks at the line once every 3.3 millisecond to see if a 1 or a 0 is being sent. Normally this sampling of the line is carried out in the middle of each bit rather than at the beginning or end, to make allowance for any small variations which may occur between the timing circuits of the two interface units in the computer and peripheral.

Finally one more bit is added at the end of each character. This is known as the *Stop* bit and gives the interface unit time to completely process the character that has just been received before the next character arrives. Thus, a total of 10 bits are used for each character so that at 300 baud, 30 characters are transmitted every second. Note that at 110 baud, 2 stop bits are used to give additional response time. The transmission for the character A is shown in Fig. 8.11.

Asynchronous serial interfaces are currently implemented in LSI technology and a brief description of currently available chips is given in Chapter 9.

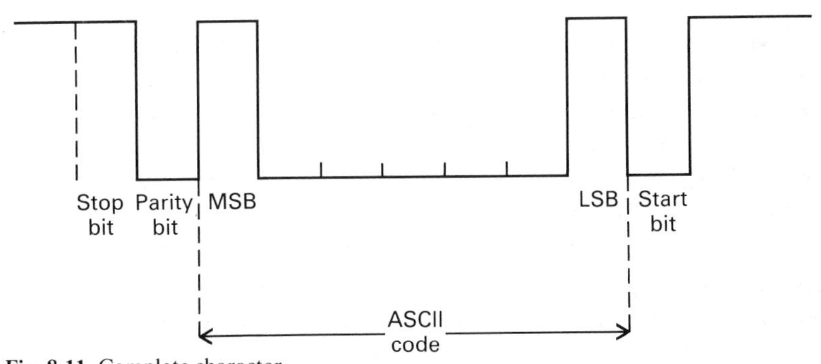

Fig. 8.11. Complete character.

Synchronous serial interfaces

In synchronous transmission the data transfer rate is determined by the system clocking. The transmitter and receiver must be synchronized with each other.

This is usually achieved by starting each message with a known synchronization code which is used by the receiver to synchronize its clock to that of the transmitter. This technique is normally used for high speed transfer of blocks of data, rather than individual characters.

Chapter 9

Large Scale Integrated Circuits

9.1 INTRODUCTION

As semiconductor technologies have developed the number of transistors that can be integrated on a single chip of silicon has rapidly increased. In the early 1950s logic gates were implemented using discrete transistors. It soon became possible to put several transistors on a single silicon chip, giving rise to *integrated circuits*, and a production process which has since become known as *small scale* integrated circuit technology (SSI). Many of the chips described in this book such as the 7400 quad two input NAND gate are in this category and are still very widely used today. By the 1960s the number of transistors on each chip had risen to several hundred using new techniques known as *medium scale* integrated circuit technology (MSI). Ten years later several thousand transistors were being packed on a chip and *large scale* integrated circuits (LSI) had arrived. Using this new MOS technology complete cental processing units were produced on a single chip and the microprocessor revolution had started. It is important to realize that the architecture of the computer did not change radically with these developments. The circuits described in the book form the basis of all processors, and are combined together on a single chip in a microprocessor.

Due to technological limitations early microprocessors, such as the Intel 4004, were only able to have 4-bit word lengths. As the technology improved 8-bit microprocessors were developed rapidly becoming an industry standard in a wide variety of application areas. 8-bit microprocessors are still in widespread use and for reasons of cost and simplicity will remain so despite the development of 16- and 32-bit microprocessors.

This chapter describes both 8-bit microprocessors and some of the support chips that go into making up a compatible family of devices.

9.2 8-BIT MICROPROCESSORS

There are a large number of different types of 8-bit microprocessors on the market today. They are incorporated in a vast range of products, ranging from toys and games to very sophisticated business data processing systems.

The unique architecture of each family of microprocessors has resulted in a number of different machine code instruction sets. The major differences between processors can be examined in two ways, firstly by looking at the external pins available on the chip itself, and secondly by defining a 'programmers model' of the register structure within the chip.

The external pins can normally be split into three major groups, known as the data bus, the address bus and the control bus. A simplified block diagram is shown in Fig. 9.1.

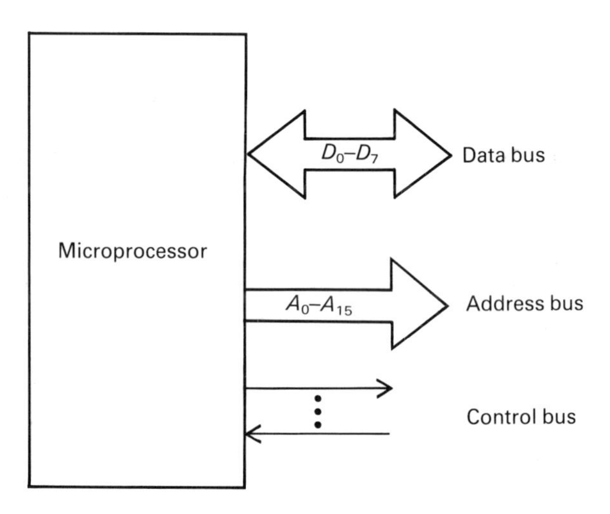

Fig. 9.1. Microprocessor bus connections.

The data and the address bus lines are standard time between different manufacturers and it is only the control bus which varies greatly. A detailed analysis of all of the control lines is beyond the scope of this book, but certain important features are discussed.

Two popular 8-bit processors, the Motorola M6800 and the Zilog Z80 are examined in this way in Sections 9.4 and 9.6.

The data bus

The number of lines in this bus classify the microprocessor as either a 4-bit, 8-bit or 16-bit device. An 8-bit microprocessor therefore has an eight-line data bus. Each line is normally *bidirectional*, in other words it can be used to transfer data into or out of the processor. The bus is used to transfer data between the processor and other chips in the system, for example, a memory chip or an interface chip.

The address bus

This bus determines how many bytes of data the system can have in its memory, It is standard to have sixteen address lines with an 8-bit data bus. This gives a maximum of 65,536 bytes (2^{16}) that can be individually addressed by the microprocessor. For many applications this amount of memory is more than sufficient. This bus is unidirectional. The address is put on the bus lines by the microprocessor and always travels away from it to the memory and interface chips.

The control bus

The lines in this bus differ widely from one microprocessor to another and have to be specified in detail for a specific manufacturer's product. However, certain general concepts do apply and the more important of these are discussed below.

The Clock. This runs at a fixed number of cycles per second (hertz). Normally a frequency somewhere between 1 and 10 megahertz (10^7 hertz) is used. It determines the speed with which the microprocessor can execute machine code instructions. Simple instructions, such as rotate accumulator, may require only two clock pulses, and would, therefore, be completed in 2 μsec (microseconds) at a clock frequency of 1 megahertz. Other more complex instructions may take over ten clock pulses to be executed.

Read/Write. These control lines determine the direction of flow of the data on the data bus. The microprocessor decides which way it wants the data to travel and then sets these lines accordingly.

Reset. This line is normally connected to an external switch of some type, possibly the normal *on/off* switch for the computer. It sends a signal into the microprocessor that forces it into a pre-defined restart procedure.

9.3 8-BIT MICROCOMPUTERS

A microcomputer consists of a microprocessor, memory and interface chips. The interface and memory chips are connected to the micro-

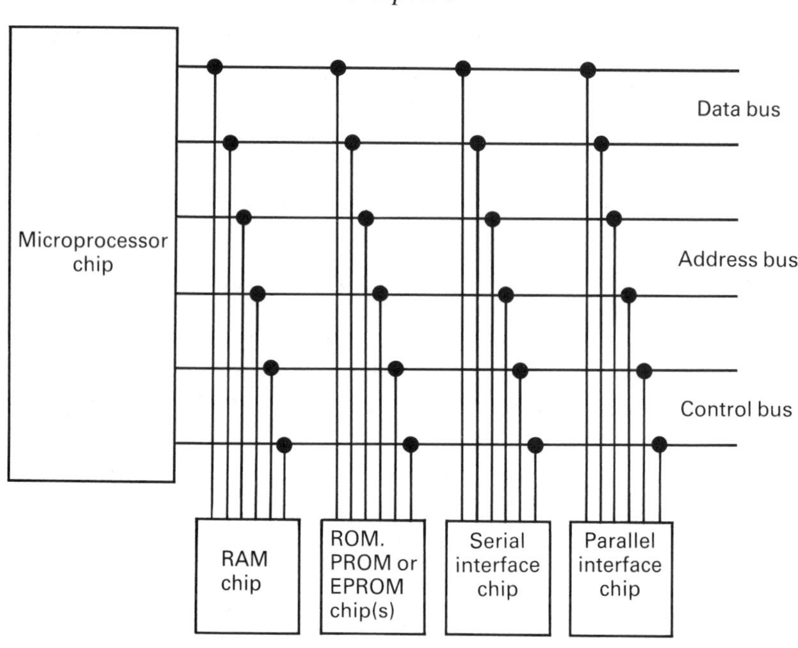

Fig. 9.2. Microcomputer block diagram.

processor using the three groups of bus lines described above and a typical configuration is shown in Fig. 9.2.

The two most common types of memory chips are random access memory (RAM) and read only memory (ROM). Both types are available from a number of manufacturers with varying characteristics such as the number of bytes per chip and access time (the time taken to access the data stored on the chip). Typical examples of these chips are given in Sections 9.7 and 9.8.

Due to packaging constraints the memory and interface chips do not have sixteen pins available for address lines, and additional decoding circuitry is sometimes required between the address bus and these chips (cf. Section 9.7 'Static RAM').

The interface chips fall into two main categories, parallel and serial. They work much the same way as the interfaces described in Chapter 8. All of the logic gates are now integrated onto one LSI chip which connects directly onto the microprocessor buses.

A parallel interface chip will transfer all 8 bits of data to or from the data bus at the same time. When the microprocessor is transferring data to the outside world, information is only available on the data bus for a few microseconds. The interface must take this information and hold it until it has been processed by the external device.

A serial interface must also accept information from the data bus in a few microseconds but it then serially shifts the data out to the peripheral device.

Examples of standard interface chips are given in Section 9.8.

9.4 MOTOROLA M6800 MICROPROCESSOR

This was the first 8-bit microprocessor produced by Motorola and more sophisticated versions such as the M6802 are now available. However, it is sensible to describe the M6800 first and then discuss the advantages of the more recent chips.

A simplified register structure is shown in Fig. 9.3. This shows only the registers that the programmer can manipulate with machine code instructions and is known as the programmer's model of the processor.

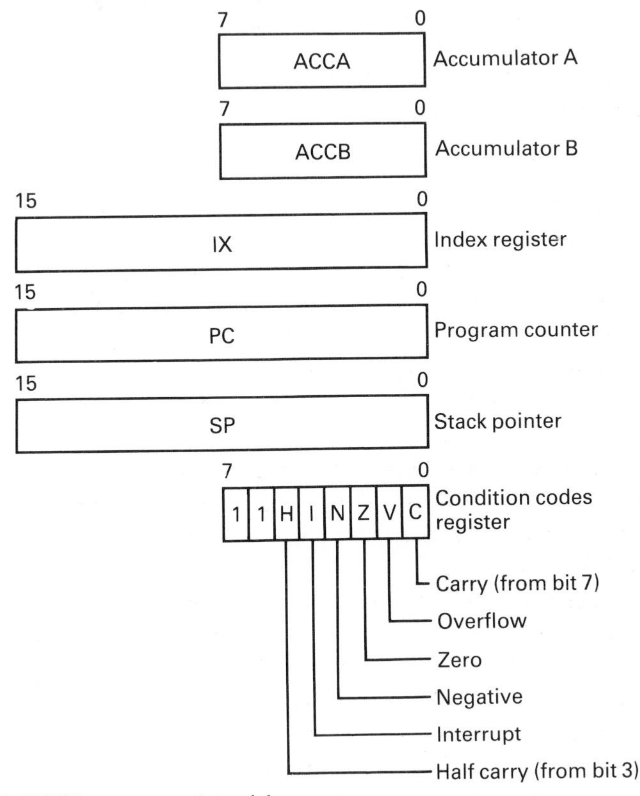

Fig. 9.3. M6800 programmer's model.

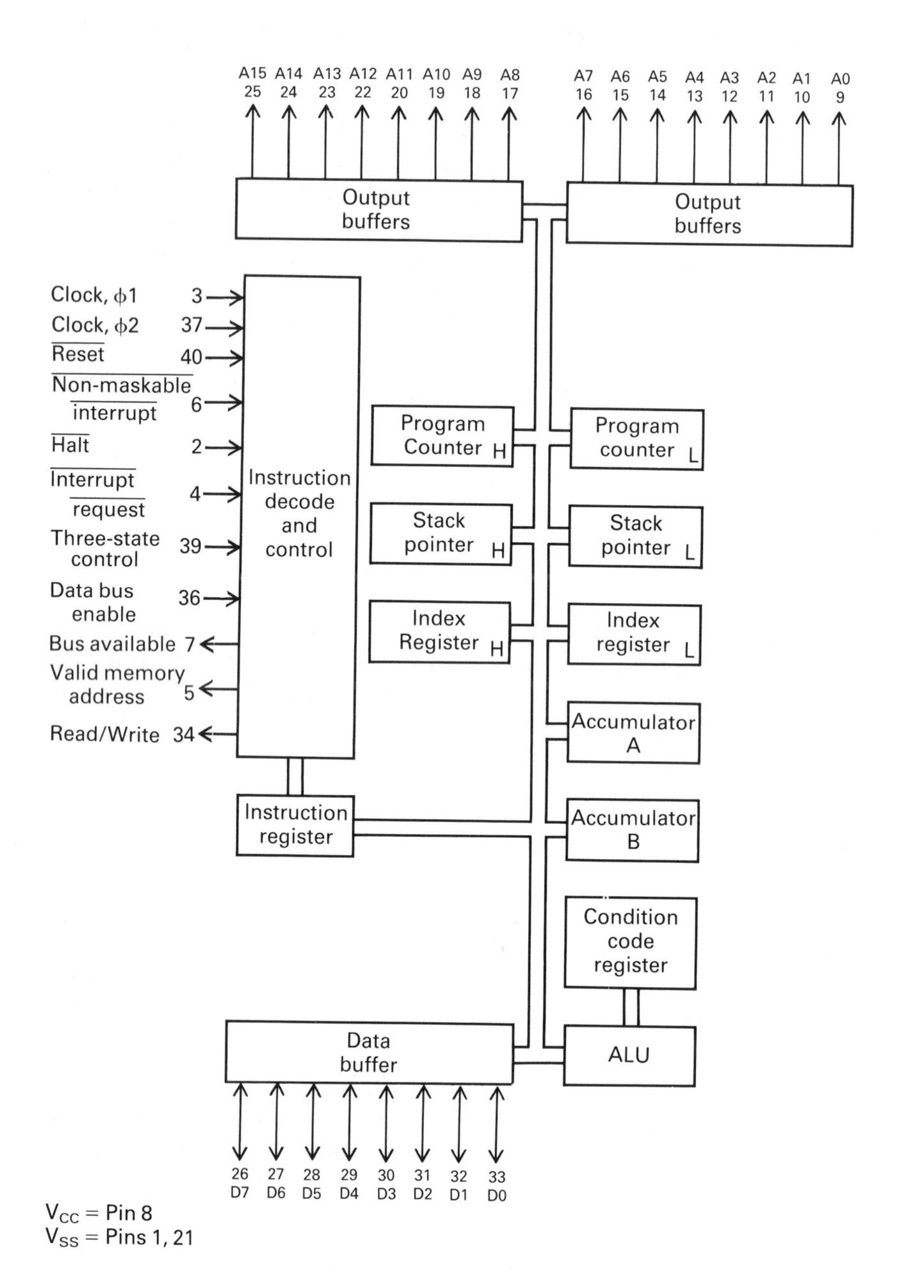

Fig. 9.4. M6800 block diagram.

The accumulators A and B are both 8-bit registers and are used to store and manipulate single bytes of data. The program counter, index register and stack pointer are all 16-bit registers used in different ways to access data stored in memory. Finally, the conditions code register is a collection of 6 bits indicating the state of the processor at any time.

A block diagram showing the internal structure and the pin connections is given in Fig. 9.4. The clock is split into two phases $\phi 1$ and $\phi 2$, where $\phi 1$ is used to read instructions and $\phi 2$ to control data transfers.

The read and write control signals are combined onto a single line with a read operation occuring when it is high and a write operation when it is low.

The reset line is active when low, indicated by the line over the word Reset in Fig. 9.4.

The remaining control lines are defined fully in Motorola's documentation.

9.5 MOTOROLA 6802 MICROPROCESSOR

This is a refinement of the M6800 chip and provides its own clock circuit and 128 bytes of RAM. These features are very useful in minimizing the number of chips required in many applications, thus reducing the overall system cost. A block diagram is shown in Fig. 9.5 (see p. 110).

9.6 ZILOG Z80 MICROPROCESSOR

This popular chip has a very different register set and control bus structure to the M6800. The register set is shown in Fig. 9.6 (see p. 111) and the pin connections in Fig. 9.7 (see p. 112).

Data is held and manipulated in the 8-bit general purpose registers. The index registers, the stack pointer and the program counter are again used to access the data in memory.

A single phase clock is fed in on CLK. The read and write control signals are separated and use the two control lines $\overline{RD}$ and $\overline{WR}$. When $\overline{RD}$ is low the processor will read the data bus and when $\overline{WR}$ is low it will write to it.

9.7 RANDOM ACCESS MEMORIES (RAM)

Information is read from, or written to these devices by the microprocessor using the data bus.

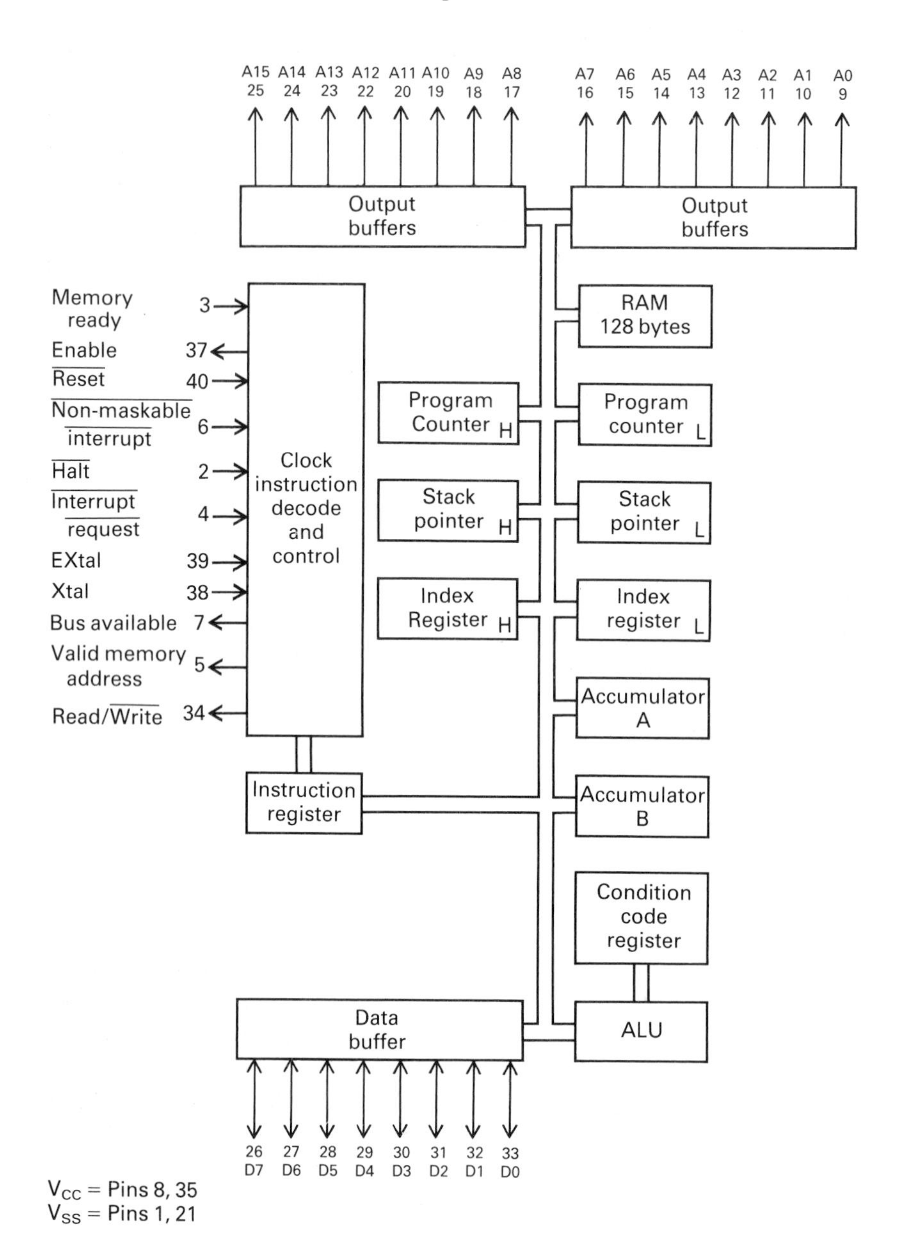

Fig. 9.5. The M6802 Microprocessor.

MAIN REGISTER SET		ALTERNATE REGISTER SET	
A ACCUMULATOR	F FLAG REGISTER	A* ACCUMULATOR	F* FLAG REGISTER
B GENERAL PURPOSE	C GENERAL PURPOSE	B* GENERAL PURPOSE	C* GENERAL PURPOSE
D GENERAL PURPOSE	E GENERAL PURPOSE	D* GENERAL PURPOSE	E* GENERAL PURPOSE
H GENERAL PURPOSE	L GENERAL PURPOSE	H* GENERAL PURPOSE	L* GENERAL PURPOSE

←8 BITS→

←16 BITS→

IX INDEX REGISTER	
IY INDEX REGISTER	
SP STACK POINTER	
PC PROGRAM COUNTER	
I INTERRUPT VECTOR	R MEMORY REFRESH

←8 BITS→

Fig. 9.6. Z80 register system.

RAM chips retain information stored in them provided the power supply is kept on. If power is switched off then all the information stored in them is lost. There are two main types of RAM devices, static and dynamic. Dynamic RAM must be periodically refreshed, approximately every 2 milliseconds, to avoid data being lost. This is an overhead that reduces system efficiency. Memory cells, can however, be packed more densely on a dynamic RAM than on a static RAM. Much more data can therefore be stored, making this a more cost effective chip.

Static RAM

A typical static RAM chip is the 4118, the pin connections of which are shown in Fig. 9.8.

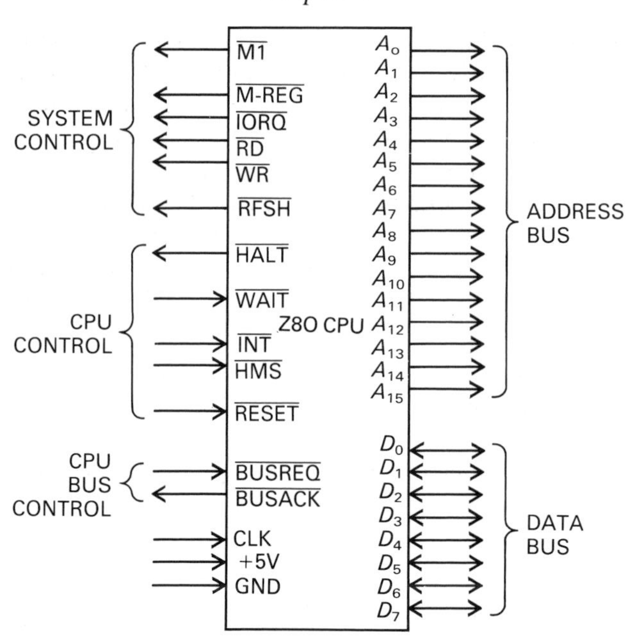

Fig. 9.7. Z80 pin connections.

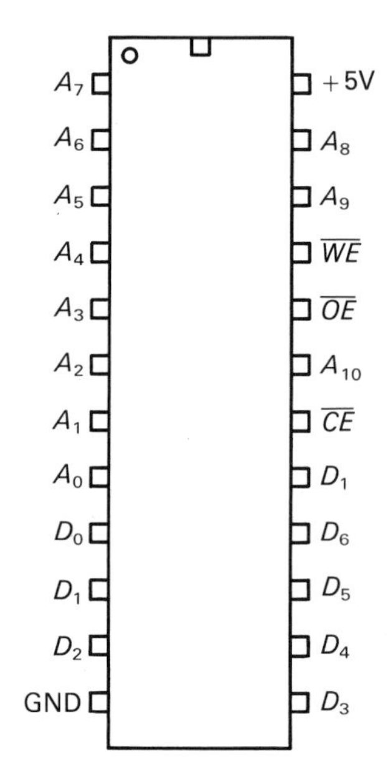

Fig. 9.8. Static RAM pin connectors (4118).

The address lines $A_0 - A_{10}$ allow each of the 1024 bytes on the chip to have a unique address. If, however, several identical chips are used in a system, only one chip must be selected at once. This can be achieved by connecting the chip enable input, $\overline{\text{CE}}$, to the remaining address lines A_{11}–A_{15}, through a decoder circuit as shown in Fig. 9.9.

This decoder circuit permits a maximum of thirty-two memory chips to be used in the system. The RAM chip connected to output 0 on the decoder is selected when all of the address bus A_{11}–A_{15} are at logical 0. The remaining chips are selected when the appropriate address is present.

The write enable input $\overline{\text{WE}}$ must be set low by the microprocessor before data can be written into the chip and set high before it can be read. The output enable pin, $\overline{\text{OE}}$, is an additional timing control signal which when set low, connects the data from the internal memory cells to the external data pins D_0–D_7.

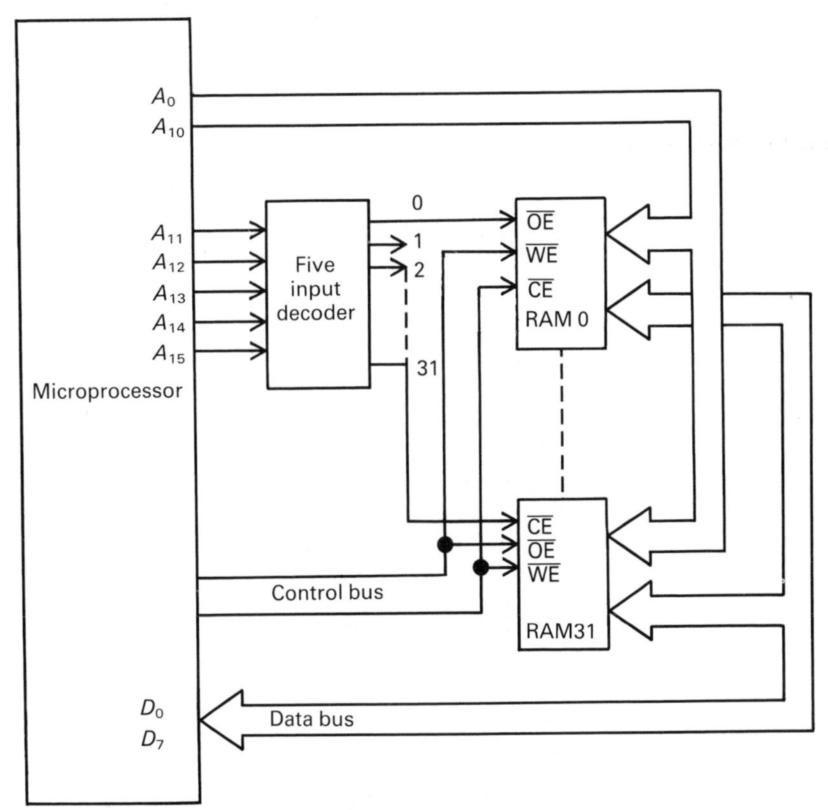

Fig. 9.9. Typical memory chip bus connections.

The data pins on the RAM chip are connected directly to the data bus of the microprocessor and the address pins to the A_0–A_{10} bus lines.

Dynamic RAM

The pin connections on dynamic RAM are similar to those on a static RAM. Two additional pins $\overline{RAS}$ (row address strobe) and $\overline{CAS}$ (column address strobe) are used to enable the address to be presented in two halves on one set of pins. The $\overline{RAS}$ pin is also used to refresh the chip. A typical device is the 4116 which is organized as a 16k × 1-bit memory (cf. Fig. 9.10). For memory to be organized in bytes eight of these chips have to be wired in parallel.

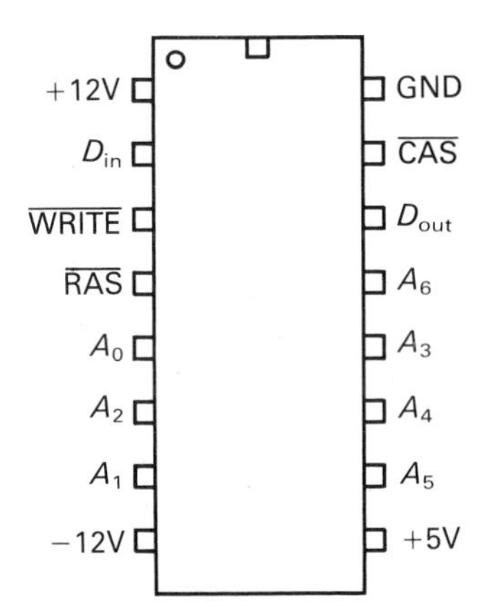

Fig. 9.10. Dynamic RAM pin connections (4116).

9.8 READ ONLY MEMORIES (ROM)

Information can only be read from this chip, and not written to it under normal operating conditions. Information is normally written into the chip before it is inserted into the microcomputer system, and once written cannot be lost when the power is switched off. This provides a non-volatile memory. The way in which ROM's are programmed divides them into several categories.

Masked ROM

The information is entered into the memory cells when the device is being manufactured and can never be altered. This is only done when a large number of identical chips are required.

Programmable read only memory (PROM)

These devices can be programmed by the user, provided specialized equipment is used. Blank PROMS can be purchased and the information entered using a process which is rather like blowing fuses. Once the data has been entered it cannot be changed.

Eraseable programmable read only memory (EPROM)

Information can only be written to the chip before it is plugged into the microcomputer system. The equipment used to program these chips is known as an EPROM programmer.

If the information in the EPROM needs changing, at any time, the chip can be removed from the system and exposed to high intensity ultra-violet light, which will completely erase the contents. The chip can then be reprogrammed.

A typical device is the 2532 chip which stores 4096 bytes of data. The pin layout of this chip is shown in Fig. 9.11.

The address and data bus connections are identical to those of the Ram chip shown in Fig. 9.9, but of course no READ/WRITE line is required.

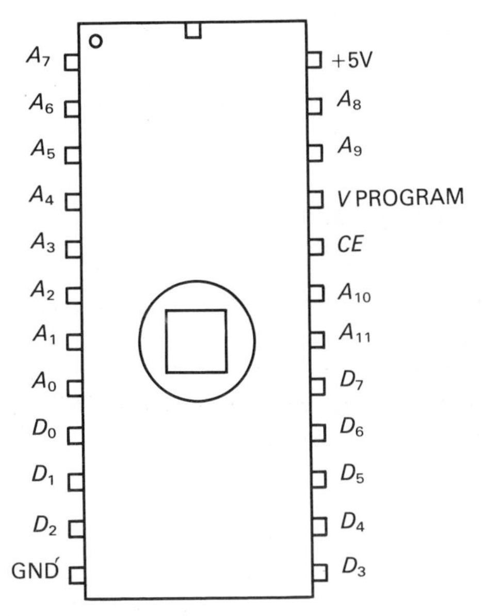

Fig. 9.11. Pin connections for EPROM 2532 chip.

9.9 INTERFACE CHIPS

The two main types of LSI interface chips are the parallel interface and the serial interface. These chips are both programmable and are widely used in interfacing peripheral devices to microcomputer systems.

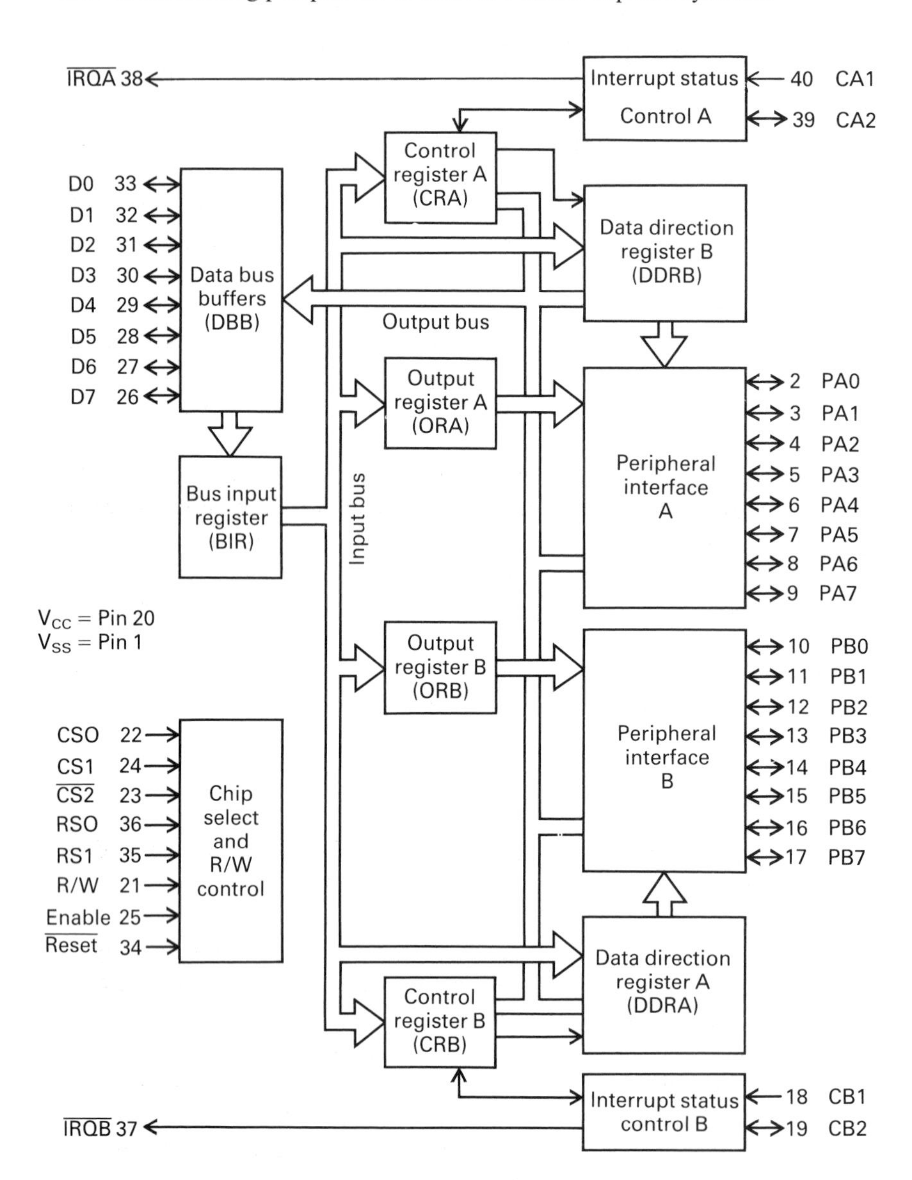

Fig. 9.12. Motorola M6821 Peripheral Interface Adaptor.

Parallel interfaces

A typical chip is the Motorola M6821 Peripheral Interface Adaptor (PIA). The main features of which are shown in Fig. 9.12.

The M6821 consists of two separate ports on one chip, each with 8 data bits and two control lines. The port connections are all TTL compatible and can be set up as input or output lines under software control using the data direction register. Each port has a control register and a data register which enable the microprocessor to communicate with, and control, both the chip and an external device. The microprocessor treats this chip as though it was a simple memory chip with a very small number of addresses corresponding to the registers. Addressing is, therefore, very similar to that described previously. The address lines A_0 and A_1 are however, replaced by the register select lines $RS0$ and $RS1$.
address lines A_0 and A_1 are however, replaced by the register select lines RS0 and RS1.

When the microprocessor transfers data to this device it is latched (frozen) by the port and can then be read by the external device. The device may indicate to the interface that it has read the data by using the control lines provided. The next item of data can then be transferred. When the external device is sending data to the microprocessor it places the required bit pattern on the input lines to the port and may again use the CA1 and CA2 lines to control the transfer. The microprocessor then reads in the data and processes it.

Similar chips are provided by all major microprocessor manufacturers (e.g. the Zilog PIO chip).

Serial interfaces

The Motorola M6850 Asynchronous Communications Interface Adaptor (ACIA) is a typical example of a serial interface. A block diagram of this chip is shown in Fig. 9.13.

It provides a serial input and a serial output channel for use by an external device, such as a visual display unit. There are four registers within the chip, a status register, a control register, a transmit data register and a receive data register. These enable the microprocessor to communicate with, and control the operation of, the chip and the peripheral in a similar way to that adopted by the PIA.

Once again similar chips are produced for other microcomputer families, (e.g. the Zilog SIO chip).

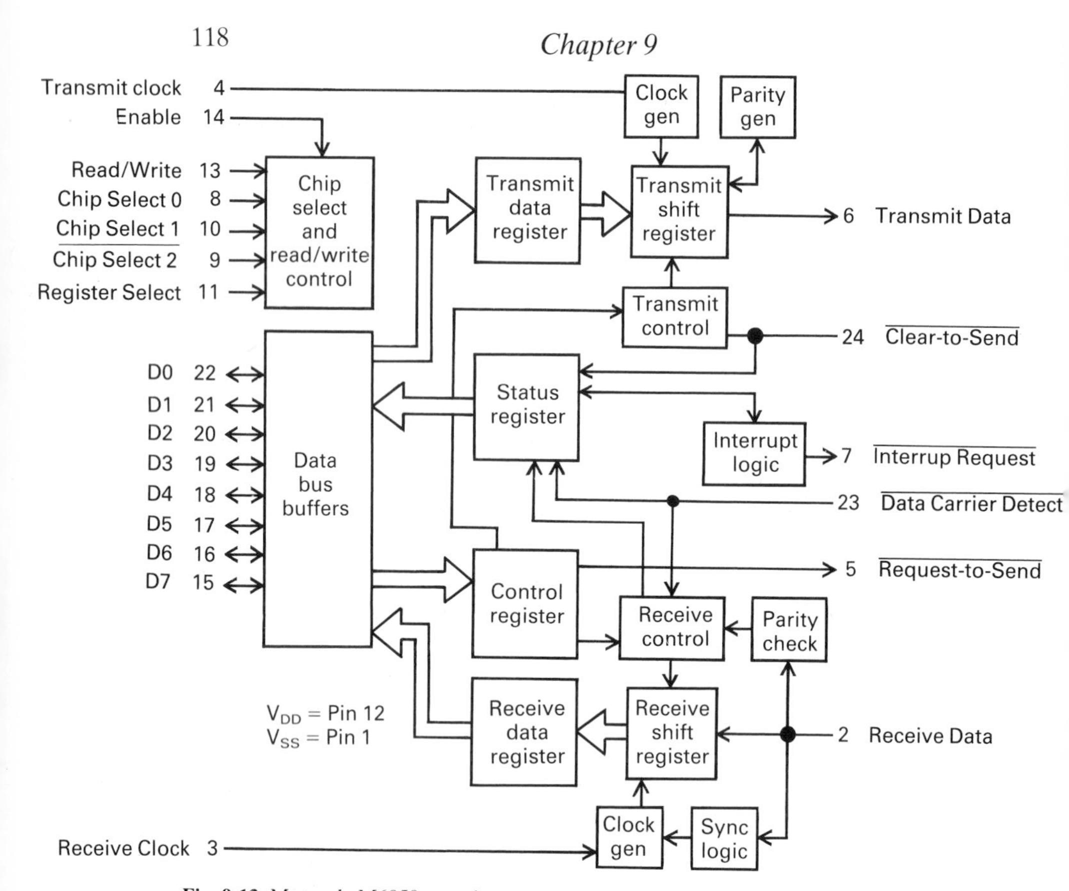

Fig. 9.13. Motorola M6850 asynchronous serial interface.

9.10 THE FUTURE

Today 16-bit microprocessors are in general use. As well as having a 16-bit data bus they have a much larger address capacity, which is of the order of many megabytes. Several manufacturers have recently announced 32-bit microprocessors which rival some mainframes in computing power, and this continual expansion of power is likely to continue for many years to come.

Considerable advances have also been made with the advent of the single chip microcomputer. This is a chip on which a microprocessor, memory and interface, are combined. Currently the amount of memory is limited to about 4k of ROM and 128 bytes of RAM, but the memory capacity will increase as this type of chip is developed. These low cost microcomputers are ideal for inclusion in a vast range of equipment, where in the past the use of a computer has not been cost effective.

Appendix 1

Transistor–Transistor Logic (TTL)

SIGNAL LEVELS

TTL logic circuits have a binary 0 defined as being approximately 0 volts and a binary 1 as being approximately +5 volts. The actual TTL chips are designed to have tolerances around these values as shown in Fig. A1.1, for example, an input to a TTL gate will be recognized as a 1 if it is between 2.0 volts and 5.0 volts, and as a 0 if it is between 0 and 0.8 volts.

The number of inputs that can be driven from one output is known as the fan-out of a chip. Most TTL outputs will drive ten inputs, in other words the fan-out of a TTL chip is 10.

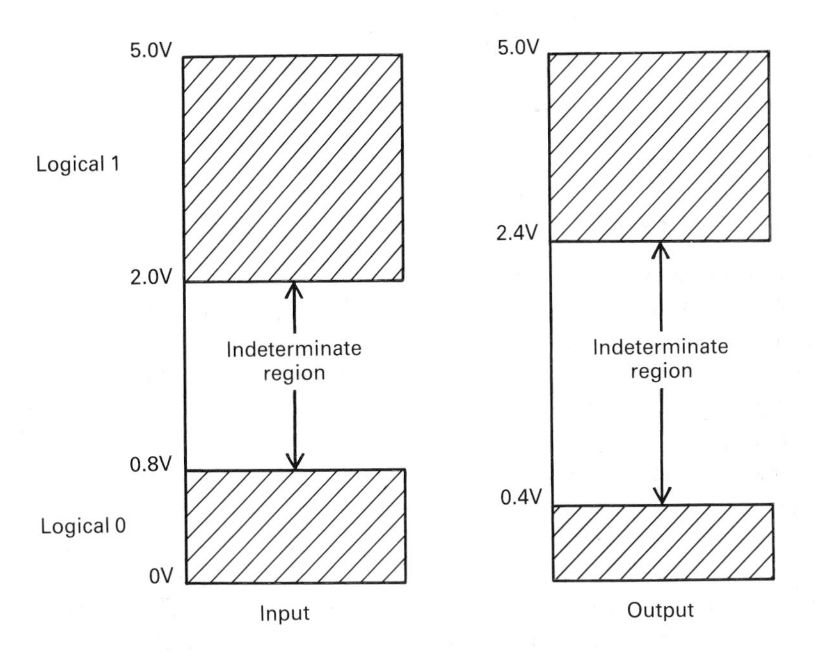

Fig. A1.1. TTL levels.

TTL LOGIC GATE

TTL logic gates are made up of a number of individual components, transistors, diodes and resistors on a single chip of silicon. The various components are connected to form the required circuit by means of a conducting material which is deposited on the chip.

Figure A1.2 shows the TTL implementation of a two input NAND gate.

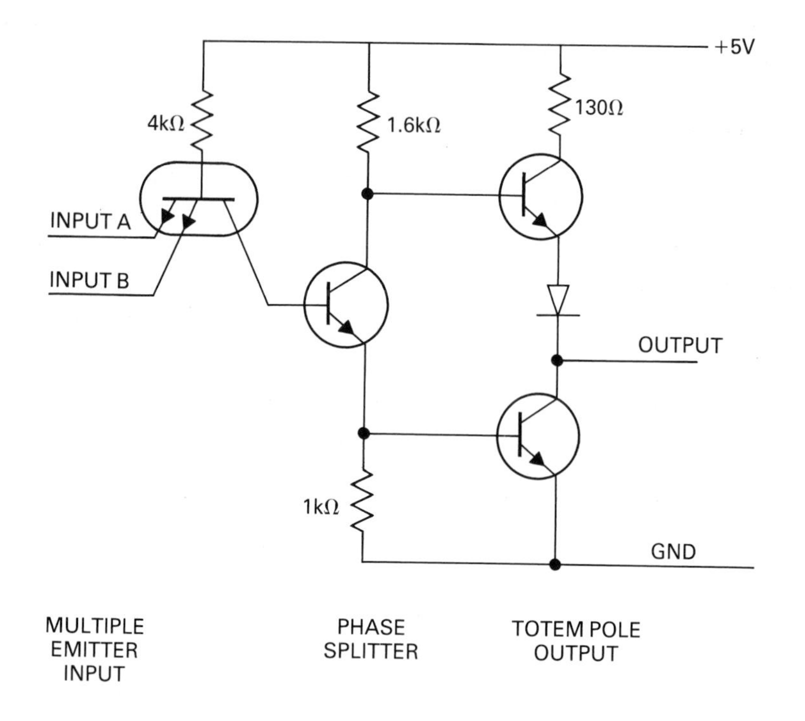

Fig. A1.2. A two input NAND gate.

TTL LOGIC CHIPS

TTL gates are used in small-scale and medium-scale integrated circuit chips in either 14 pin, 16 pin or 20 pin packages. The pins are numbered counter clockwise starting from the notch in one end of the chip. Each chip has a number identifying it printed on the top. Figure A1.3 shows the pin layout for an 74LS00 Quad two-input NAND gate chip.

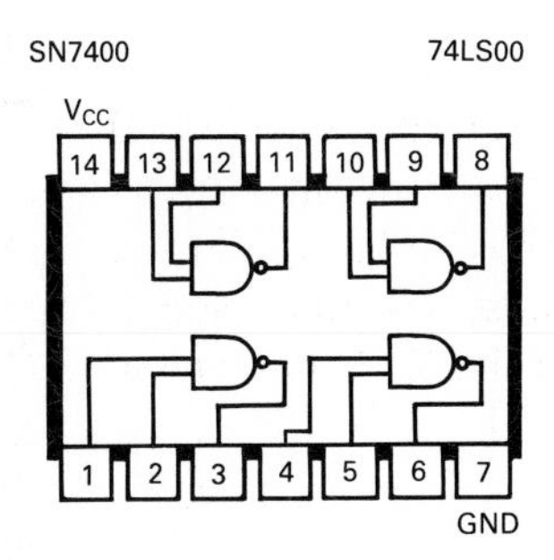

Fig. A1.3. Quad two input NAND gate.

LOGIC FAMILIES

There are a vast variety of different chips produced in several different technologies each having its own power and propagation delay characteristics. Figure A1.4 summarizes current logic families and their global characteristics.

Figure A1.5 (see p. 122) shows the layouts of some of the chips in any of the logic families.

Family	Typical gate propagation delay	Typical power dissipation per gate (mW)	
74 LS XXX	10	2	General purpose TTL
74 S XXX	3	19	Fast TTL
74 ALS XXX	5	1	Advanced versions of 74 LS and 74 S families.
74 AS XXX	1.5	22	

Fig. A1.4. TTL families.

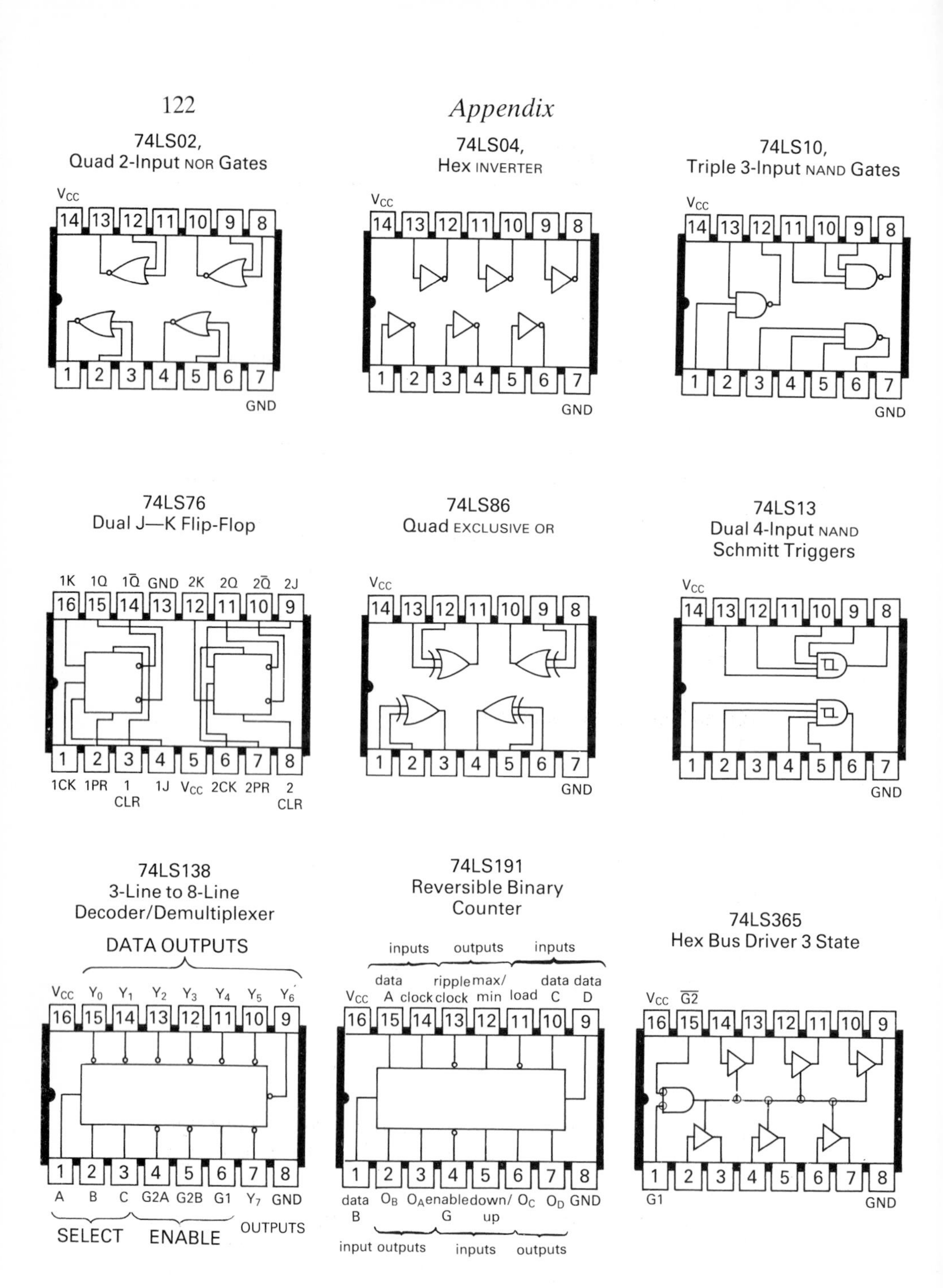

Fig. A1.5. Pin layouts.

Appendix 2

Building the Logic Tutor

The practical work described in Appendix 3 and the majority of examples used throughout this book can be built with a minimum number of chips on the logic tutor described below.

To build the tutor the following components are required:

1 Printed circuit board. Vero No. 10-0156 or Radio Spares No. RS434-021
1 8-way DIL switch block. Radio Spares No. RS337-560
1 10-bar DIL LED array. Radio Spares No. RS586-706
7 14-pin DIL integrated circuit sockets
5 16-pin DIL integrated circuit sockets
2 74LS00 Quad 2 input NAND gates
2 74LS04 Hex inverters
1 74LS86 Quad 2 input EXCLUSIVE OR
1 74LS10 Triple 3 input NAND gates
2 74LS76 Dual J.K. Flip Flop
1 74LS365 Hex tri-state buffer
1 74LS191 Binary Counter
1 74LS138 3 to 8 Decoder/Multiplexer
1 74LS13 Dual 4 Input NAND Schmitt Triggers
1 470 μF Capacitor (small)—C1
1 560 Ω resistor —R1
1 10 kΩ SIL resistor network
280 pins Cambion Part No. 155-1048-01-04-00
12 wires Cambion Part No. 445-3663-04-03-10 (long)
12 wires Cambion Part No. 445-3663-02-03-12 (med)
12 wires Cambion Part No. 445-3663-01-03-10 (short)

The only tools needed to build the logic tutor are a fine tipped soldering iron, and solder, a pair of small pliers and a pair of wire cutters/strippers.

Figure A2.1 shows the layout of the printed circuit board and the DIL integrated circuit sockets which should be soldered in place on the component mounting side of the board. The eight-way DIL switches and the ten-bar DIL LED display should then be positioned as shown and soldered into place on the same side of the board.

Bared wire straps should next be inserted on the component side of the board between the switches and the earth (ground) rail and the displays and the earth rail, as shown in Fig. A2.1. The straps should be soldered into place.

The eight-way SIL resistor network should be positioned with the common pin (marked by a dot) one hole to the left of the switch pack, and link made between this position and the +5 volt rail.

The next stage in building the tutor is to make a clock unit for use with the sequential logic chips. The clock uses the SN7413 Dual 4 input NAND Schmitt trigger chip and the capacitor C1 and resistor R1 which have to be inserted on the component side of the board and soldered into place.

Next the pins used to connect the various integrated circuits have to be put in the positions shown in Fig. A2.1. The pins are inserted through the wiring side of the board, narrow end first, and lightly pulled into position from the component mounting side with a pair of small pliers. Each pin is then soldered in place.

The two wires to the battery or 5 volt power supply are then soldered onto the pins as shown in the diagram and the integrated circuits positioned with pin 1 to the bottom left as illustrated. The board is now ready for testing and use.

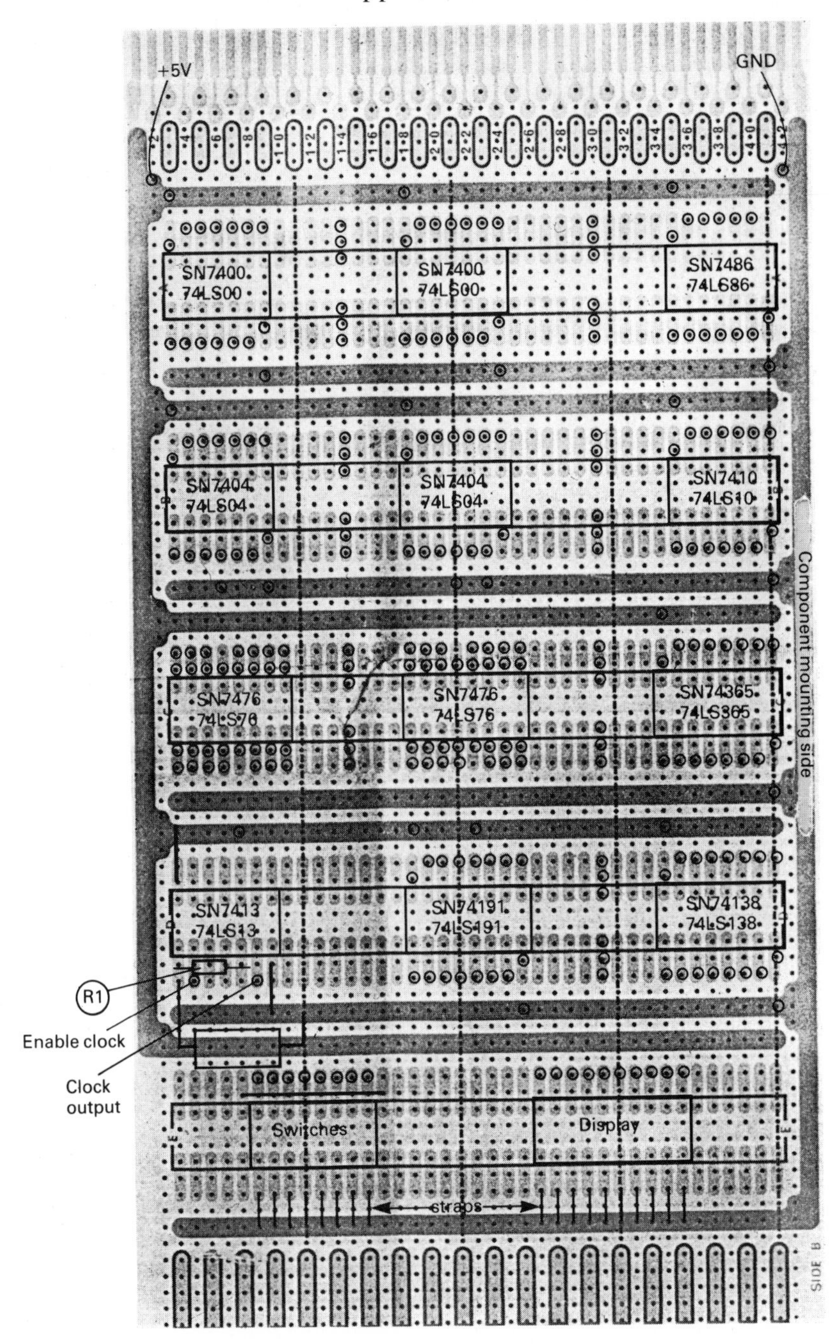

Fig. A2.1. The layout of the Logic Tutor.

Appendix 3

A Practical Course on the Logic Tutor

INTRODUCTION

Before introducing the practical course, two cautionary notes:

(i) do not connect +5 volt (Vcc) directly to the displays or they may burn out, and

(ii) Always disconnect the +5 volt wire from the battery or power supply when wiring up or disconnecting the board.

TESTING THE CLOCK

Test the clock by connecting the clock output pin to any of the display pins with one of the wires. The selected display should then flash about once a second when the +5 volt wire is connected to the battery or power supply. If it does not, disconnect the +5 volt wire and check all connections and soldering.

The enable clock pin can be connected to one of the switch pins and the selected switch used to start and stop the clock pulses.

A PRACTICAL COURSE

The practical work is based on the Contents and examples of Chapters 1, 2, 4 to 6, and 8.

CHAPTER 1 TTL LOGIC GATES

1.1 Inverter SN7404

Connect a wire between V_{cc} (pin 14) on one of the SN7404 chips and the +5 volt rail. Connect a second wire between GND (pin 7) on the same chip and the GND rail. Connect one of the switches to pin 1 of the chip and the output from pin 2 to one of the LEDS.

With the switch nearest the bottom of the board a 0 is input to the inverter (switch up) and a 1 can be seen to be output as the display is on. Changing the switch position to input a 1 (down) will make the output a 0 and the display will be turned off.

Disconnect the power and then disconnect the circuit. Each of the other inverters on the chip can be tested by moving the wire from the switch to the input and the wire to the display to the output of each gate in turn and operating the switch with the battery connected.

1.2 Two input NAND gate SN7400

Connect up the V_{cc} and GND (pins 14 and 7 respectively) of a SN7400 chip to the appropriate supply rail.

Connect a switch to each of the two inputs of one of the gates and the output of that gate to one of the displays. (The layout of the chip is given in Appendix 1).

Verify the truth table given in Fig. 1.15.

1.3 Three input NAND gate SN7410

Repeat 1.2 above using a three input NAND gate and draw the truth table.

1.4 Two input exclusive OR SN7486

In a similar way verify the truth table for a two input EXCLUSIVE OR gate given in Fig. 1.16.

CHAPTER 2 THE ANALYSIS AND DESIGN OF LOGICAL CIRCUITS

2.1 Two input NOR gate

Connect up the circuit for a NOR gate derived in Example 2.1 of the main text and shown in Fig. 2.7 as follows:

(i) Connect the V_{cc} and GND to both SN7404 and SN7400 chip.

(ii) Connect two switches to inputs on separate inverters.

(iii) Connect the outputs from the INVERTERS to the inputs of a NAND gate on the SN7400 chip.

(iv) Connect the output from the NAND to the input of an INVERTER and the output from the INVERTER to one of the LEDs.

Verify that this circuit is a NOR gate by going through the four combinations of inputs on the switches and drawing a truth table, which should correspond to Fig. 2.6.

2.2 Two input exclusive OR

Build the circuit for the two input EXCLUSIVE OR gate shown in Fig. 2.11.

2.3 Two pairs of inputs

Build the circuit shown in Fig. 2.13 and verify its operation by drawing a truth table.

2.4 Boolean algebra

Label the following circuit diagram showing the Boolean expressions at each point on the circuit.

Draw a truth table showing the two outputs for each of the combinations of the three inputs (cf. Fig. A3.1).

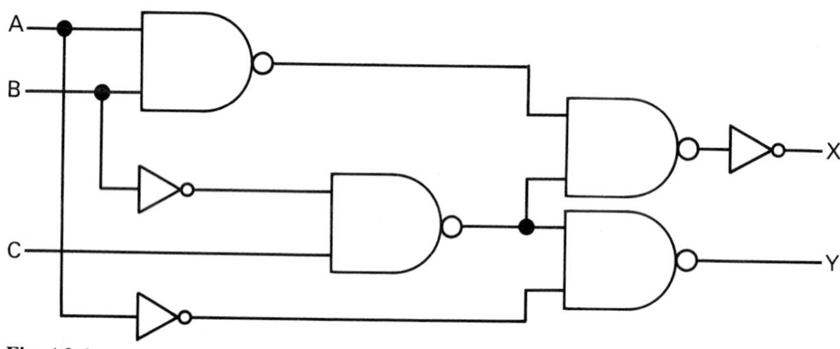

Fig. A3.1

Connect up the circuit and verify the truth table.

2.5 Example from Karnaugh maps

(i) Connect up the circuit diagram given in Fig. 2.26 and verify its truth table given in Table 2.8.

(ii) Build the circuit shown in Fig. 2.29 and prove the truth table. (Table 2.9). A three input NAND gate has to be built from two two-input NAND gates and an INVERTER.

2.6 Karnaugh maps

Using Karnaugh maps and Boolean algebra design the build circuits, using NAND gates and INVERTERS only, to perform the operations specified in the truth tables below (cf. Tables A2.1 and A2.2).

Table A2.1

A	*B*	*C*	Output
0	0	0	0
0	0	1	1
0	1	0	0
0	1	0	0
1	0	1	1
1	0	0	0
1	1	1	1
1	1	0	0

Table A2.2

A	*B*	*C*	*D*	Output
0	0	0	0	1
0	0	0	1	1
0	0	1	0	1
0	0	1	1	0
0	1	0	0	1
0	1	0	1	0
0	1	1	0	1
0	1	1	1	0
1	0	0	0	1
1	0	0	1	1
1	0	1	0	1
1	0	1	1	0
1	1	0	0	0
1	1	0	1	0
1	1	1	0	0
1	1	1	1	0

CHAPTER 4 THE ARITHMETIC AND LOGIC UNIT

4.1 Half-adder

(i) Connect up the circuit for a half-adder shown in Fig. 4.2. Check that it correctly adds the two single bit numbers (A_0 and B_0) together and compare the outputs obtained with the expected results given in Table 4.1. NAND gates and INVERTERS must be used to replace the AND and OR gates.

(ii) Prove that a simpler half-adder circuit can be obtained using an EXCLUSIVE OR gate as shown in Fig. 4.3.

4.2 Full adder

Connect the circuit for a full adder shown in Fig. 4.6. Check that it correctly adds the three single bit numbers (A_1, B_1 and C_0) together.

4.3 A two-stage subtractor

Draw a logic circuit for a two-stage binary subtraction unit.

Connect the circuit and check that it correctly performs a subtraction operation.

4.4 Comparators (equality)

(i) A comparator circuit which indicates when two binary digits are equal is shown in Fig. 4.11. Modify this circuit so that only NAND gates and INVERTERS are used in the design.

(ii) Build a two-stage comparator circuit, similar to that shown in Fig. 4.12, using only NAND gates and INVERTERS.

4.5 Comparator (Less Than or Equality)

(i) Using a Karnaugh map develop a minimized design for a two-stage comparator circuit to indicate when the number *A* is less than or equal to the number *B*.

(ii) Build and test the circuit using only NAND gates and INVERTERS.

CHAPTER 5 DECODER AND MULTIPLEXERS

5.1 A 2-to-4 decoder

Using the example shown in Fig. 5.2 design a 2-to-4 decoder circuit using NAND gates and INVERTERS.

By connecting two switches to the input address lines and LEDs on the outputs build and test the circuit.

5.2 A 3-to-8 decoder 74138

The 74138 chip in the logic tutor is a complete 3-to-8 decoder and its pin connections are shown in Fig. A1.5.

Connect three switches to the address select line *A*, *B* and *C* and eight LEDs to the outputs Y0–Y7. Then connect the enable inputs G2A and G2B to ground and G1 to a switch. Set up the required address on *A*, *B* and *C* and check that the correct output is activated when the device is enabled using the switch on G1. Note that the outputs are 1 when not selected and 0 when selected. Disable the outputs and then repeat the procedure using a different address.

5.3 A 2-bit priority encoder

Connect the circuit for a 2-bit priority encoder shown in Fig. 5.8. Check its operation by comparing the outputs obtained with the truth table shown in Table 5.3.

5.4 Multiplexers

(i) Redesign the multiplexer circuit shown in Fig. 5.11 to provide four data inputs, using only NAND gates and INVERTERS. Then indicate clearly which parts of the circuit could be replaced by the 74138 chip with the most significant address line wired to ground.

(ii) Redesign the demultiplexer circuit shown in Fig. 5.12 to provide four data outputs, using only NAND gates and INVERTERS.

(iii) Construct a data transmission system similar to that shown in Fig. 5.13, with four data inputs and outputs, using the circuits designed in parts (i) and (ii) of this question.

Test the operation of the system by connecting switches to the data input lines and to the address lines and by connecting LEDs to the data output lines. Select address 00 and check that the input data on line D_0 is transmitted through the system and appears on the correct LED, repeat this procedure for the remaining addresses.

CHAPTER 6 SEQUENTIAL LOGIC

6.1 J-K Flip Flop SN7476

(i) Connect one J-K Flip Flop on a 7476 chip by wiring switches to the *J*, *K*, *Clear* (*CLR*) and *Preset* (*PR*) pins, and LEDs to Q and $\bar{Q}$. Then wire the output pin of the 1 second clock circuit to the clock pin (*CK*) of the Flip Flop and also to another LED.

(ii) Set the initial conditions on the *Clear* and *Preset* inputs to those specified in Section 6.2, 'Initial conditions' in the main text, and check that the Q and $\bar{Q}$ outputs are correct.

(iii) Set the *Clear* and *Preset* inputs and the *J* and *K* inputs to a 1. Look at the two LEDs and check that the output Q is flashing at half the frequency of the clock, i.e. approximately once every 2 seconds. This displays the basic divide by two characteristics of the J-K Flip Flop as described in Section 6.2, 'Divide by two characteristics' in the main text.

(iv) Clear Q to 0 using the *Clear* and *Preset* inputs. Set *J* to 1 and *K* to 0 and then set *Clear* and *Preset* both to 1 again. The output Q will stay at 0 until the falling edge of the clock arrives, when it will become a 1.

This demonstrates the 1-bit storage characteristic as described in Section 6.2, '1-bit store characteristics' in the main text.

6.2 A four-stage asynchronous counter

(i) Connect up a four-stage asynchronous binary up-counter, using the circuit shown in Fig. 6.5. Clear all of the outputs to 0 using the *Clear* and *Preset* inputs. Then set the *Clear* and *Preset* switches both to 1, the binary pattern appearing on the LEDs will show a count which is incremented on the falling edge of every clock pulse.

(ii) Modify the circuit to that of a four-stage asynchronous binary down-counter as shown in Fig. 6.7. Set all of the outputs to 1 using the *Clear* and *Preset* inputs. Then set *Clear* and *Preset* back to 1 and observe the output counting down from 15 to 0.

6.3 MSI Reversible Binary Counter

Connect V_{cc} and GND to the Reversible Binary Counter 74LS191. Connect up the clock and wire four switches to the data inputs *A* to *D*. Wire switches to load (pin 11), enable (pin 4) and down/up (pin 5) and connect each output to a LED.

With enable and load both set to 1, verify that the pattern on the *A* to *D* inputs appears on the outputs. Set the down/up pin to 1 and verify that the chip counts up as soon as set to 0.

Repeat the load and run procedure with down/up set to 0 and verify that the chip counts down. Connect the ripple clock to the load and verify that the counter now counts both up and down from the initial value set on the *A* to *D* data inputs.

6.4 Parallel registers

(i) Connect the four-stage parallel register as shown in Fig. 6.13 and wire four switches to the J inputs and four LEDs to the outputs D_0–D_3. (Note, replace the AND gates with NAND gates and INVERTERS). Now connect the 1-second system clock and two enable switches, set to 0, to the circuit. With the *enable input* switch set to 1 the register will latch (freeze) the input data from the four switches, on the falling edge of the next clock pulse. If the *enable input* is now set to 0, the original date from the switches will remain stored in the register, and any new settings on the switches will have no effect. The stored data will be available on the *Q* outputs but will not reach the output data bus until the *enable output* switch is set to a 1.

(ii) Modify the circuit used in Fig. 6.13 to correspond to that shown in Fig. 6.16. Use the 74365 chip for the tri-state gates with $\overline{G2}$ connected to ground and $\overline{G1}$ to the *enable output* switch, note that a 0 on $\overline{G1}$ enables the outputs. Test the circuit in the same way as in (i) above, and note that when the outputs are disabled the data bus is floating and not tied to a logic 0 level as it was previously.

CHAPTER 8 INTERFACING

8.1 A serial-in-parallel-out register

Connect the circuit for a four-stage Serial-In-Parallel-Out register (SIPO), shown in Fig. 8.6. Wire switches to the *Clear, Preset* and *Data In* pins and LEDs to the four outputs, connect the 1-second clock to the circuit.

Clear the outputs using the *Clear* and *Preset* switches and then set them both to a 1. The data on the *Data In* pin will be entered into the stage 1 flip flop on the falling edge of the next clock pulse and will be shifted into subsequent stages on succeeding clock pulses. Hence, after four clock pulses new data will have been shifted into all four stages. The data on the *Data In* pin can be altered between clock pulses so that any binary sequence of 0's and 1's can be entered into the register.

8.2 A parallel-in-serial-out register

Connect the circuit for a four-stage Parallel-In-Serial-Out register (PISO) by adding one more stage to the circuit shown in Fig. 8.9. Wire switches to the four parallel data input lines D_0–D_3 and to the *run/load* line, also wire four LEDs to the output Q_0–Q_3.

Set up the parallel data to be loaded into the register on the input lines D_0–D_3 and set the *run/load* switch to a 1. This data should appear on the outputs Q_0–Q_3 on the falling edge of the next clock pulse. When the *run/load* switch is set to a 0 the data will be shifted one stage at a time through the register on the falling edge of every clock pulse. After four clock pulses all of the original data would have been shifted out of the Q_3 output pin.

Appendix 4

ASCII and EBCDIC Codes

4.1 ASCII code

Table A4.1

Numeric identification bits	Zone identification							
3210	000	001	010	011	100	101	110	111
0000	NULL	DC0	ƀ	0	@	P		p
0001	SOM	DC1	!	1	A	Q	a	q
0010	EOA	DC2	″	2	B	R	b	r
0011	EOM	DC3	#	3	C	S	c	s
0100	EOT	DC4	$	4	D	T	d	t
0101	WRU	ERR	%	5	E	U	e	u
0110	RU	SYNC	&	6	F	V	f	v
0111	BELL	LEM	'	7	G	W	g	w
1000	BKSP	S0	(	8	H	X	h	x
1001	HT	S1	)	9	I	Y	i	y
1010	LF	S2	*	:	J	Z	j	z
1011	VT	S3	+	;	K	[	k	{
1100	FF	S4	,	<	L	\	l	|
1101	CR	S5	–	=	M	]	m	}
1110	SO	S6	.	>	N	↑	n	ESC
1111	SI	S7	/	?	O	←	o	DEL

NULL, Null/Idle
SOM, Start of message
EOA, End of address
EOM, End of message
EOT, End of transmission
WRU, "Who are you?"
RU, "Are you . . .?"
BELL, Audible signal
BKSP, Backspace
HT, Horizontal tab
LF, Line feed
VT, Vertical tab
FF, Form feed
CR, Carriage return
SO, Shift out
SI, Shift in
DC0–DC4, Device control
ERR, Error
SYNC, Synchronous idle
LEM, Logical end of media
S0–S7, Separator information
ƀ, Blank
ESC, Escape
DEL, Delete/Idle

Format

7	6	5	4	3	2	1	0

Bit 7 = Parity.

4.2 EBCDIC code

Table A4.2

Bit positions	Bit positions 7654															
3210	0000	0001	0010	0011	0100	0101	0110	0111	1000	1001	1010	1011	1100	1101	1110	1111
0000	NULL				SP	&	–									0
0001							/		a	j			A	J		1
0010									b	k	s		B	K	S	2
0011									c	l	t		C	L	T	3
0100	PF	RES	BYP	PN					d	m	u		D	M	U	4
0101	HT	NL	LF	RS					e	n	v		E	N	V	5
0110	LC	BS	EOB	UC					f	o	w		F	O	W	6
0111	DEL	IL	PRE	EOT					g	p	x		G	P	X	7
1000									h	q	y		H	Q	Y	8
1001									i	r	z		I	R	Z	9
1010			SM		¢	!		:								
1011					.	$	,	#								
1100					<	*	%	@								
1101					(	)	–	'								
1110					+	;	>	=								
1111					|	—	?	"								

NULL, Null/Idle
PF, Punch off
HT, Horizontal tab
LC, Lower case
DEL, Delete
RES, Restore
NL, New line
BS, Backspace
IL, Idle
BYP, Bypass
LF, Line feed
EOB, End of block
PRE, Prefix
SM, Set mode
PN, Punch on
RS, Reader stop
UC, Upper case
EOT, End of transmission
SP, Space

Format	7	6	5	4	3	2	1	0

Index